YOUTHWORK AND HOW TO DO IT

YOUTHWORK
AND HOW TO DO IT

Pete Ward
Sam Adams
Jude Levermore

LYNX

Published by
Lynx Communications
an imprint of Lion Publishing plc
Peter's Way, Sandy Lane West,
Oxford OX4 5HG
ISBN 0 7459 2879 X

First edition 1994

A catalogue record for this book is
available from the British Library

Illustrations by Ivan Hissey

Printed and bound in Malta

CONTENTS

INTRODUCTION   7

1   APPROACHES TO YOUTHWORK   9

2   INTERPERSONAL SKILLS FOR YOUTHWORKERS   25

3   GROWING UP: THE INSIDE WORLD   44

4   TELLING THE GOOD NEWS   76

5   YOUTH CULTURE   89

6   GROUPS AND HOW THEY WORK   104

7   GROWING UP: THE OUTSIDE WORLD   116

8   WORSHIP AND YOUNG PEOPLE   145

INTRODUCTION

DO NOT SKIP THIS BIT!

Phew, I'm glad you've started to read this page. I promise to keep this 'Introduction' to the bare essentials.

But first let me say a big welcome from Sam, Jude and myself. We have written this guide because we think people who spend time with young people are extremely important. We have put pen to paper because we want to help and encourage you in your youthwork. Now down to those bare essentials I mentioned.

1   WHO IS THIS GUIDE FOR?

◆ Are you a youthworker meeting young people at least once a week?

◆ Do you want to think more about your work with young people?

◆ Do you want a course which includes practical exercises to help you learn?

If your answer to these questions is 'Yes' then this is the course for you.

2   HOW LONG IS THIS COURSE?

The course should take the average reader about sixteen weeks to complete. You could do this in one long haul, but we suggest that you divide the course into two equal parts of four chapters each. This should give you two equal periods of study of about eight weeks' work. In between you could have a two- or three-week holiday.

3   HOW FAST MUST I WORK?

Each chapter of this book is divided into four *sections*. We have designed these so that the average reader will take about four hours to read them and complete the exercises. We realize however that some people will work faster and some will be slower; the important thing is that you go at a pace at which you are comfortable.

4   HOW DOES THE COURSE WORK?

In each chapter you will find four general headings: 'Instructions', 'Input', 'Exercise' and 'Feedback'.

Instructions. These give you advance warning of what you have to do in each chapter. It is worth glancing at these ahead of time to see if you need particular materials to complete the work in one sitting.

NPUT

These are the main theory sections of the book which help you to think through the issues tackled in each chapter.

EXERCISE

Each section will include at least one, but probably more, exercises. In general you should be able to complete these during the four hours you have set aside to do the course each week. Occasionally the exercise will ask you to try something out with the young people you are working with.

FEEDBACK

Doing a course from a book is tough, because you can't talk to the tutor about what you are learning. Feedback is written to give some idea of what the tutor might say after you have completed the exercises.

The notebook. We suggest that you keep your work for the course in a notebook. This should probably be a loose-leaf folder.

5 CAN I DO THIS COURSE ON MY OWN?

Yes. We have written this material assuming that the reader is working mainly on their own.

6 CAN A GROUP OF YOUTHWORKERS USE THIS COURSE?

Yes, you can work on this material together. However you will need to use your imagination on how you tackle each chapter. With the exercises you could decide ahead of time if you could do these as a group, in pairs or on your own. As a group, you could perhaps agree to do the work in each chapter separately and then meet together to discuss what you have learned.

SUPPORT FOR THE YOUTHWORKER

Youthwork is a tough job and we all need support from time to time. It is tempting to think that this course will solve all your problems. Let me say now: 'It won't.' The chances are that this course will give you *more* problems because it will get you thinking and asking questions about what you are doing. In the short term you might think this is a pain in the neck, but in the long run this course will help you to develop as a youthworker. Whilst you are on the course you will need all the support that you can get.

So finally here is a checklist to help you keep going as a youthworker when you are doing the course.

1 **Tell your minister or vicar that you are doing this course.**

2 **Tell your youthwork colleagues that you are doing the course.**

3 **Find a couple of people and ask them to pray for you regularly while you are doing the youthwork and studying.**

4 **Find someone who you can talk with about the course.**

APPROACHES TO YOUTHWORK

1

Pete Ward

GETTING THE PICTURE

EXERCISE

I want you to imagine that you have just moved to a new town which has just been built. There is no youthwork happening whatsoever. You have been asked by the local churches to come up with a plan for youthwork which involves those young people who *do not* come to church on Sundays. What are you going to do?

Take about ten minutes to think about what you think the church should be doing for those young people who are outside the church.

Write this short plan in your notebooks.

FEEDBACK

Starting from scratch is a very rare thing in youthwork. Most of us inherit youthwork which already exists, or we copy work we see elsewhere. I have asked you to start with this short imaginary exercise because it focuses the mind on two questions.

◆ What is the aim of youthwork?

◆ What is the best way to achieve that aim?

This section deals with different approaches to youthwork and outlines ways that you can evaluate these approaches.

INPUT

Those of us writing this course have assumed that you, the reader, are in some way involved on a weekly basis in youthwork. What we haven't tried to guess is what kind of youthwork you are currently doing. Part of the reason for this is that there are so many different types of youthwork happening all over the country. Running a youth club and helping out with the local Scout troop are both youthwork but they are very different. Here are two thumbnail sketches to illustrate what I mean.

Jim the Sea Scout leader

Elisabeth at the youth club

Jim is a Sea Scout leader. He leads a troop of about twenty-five boys and girls aged between eleven and fifteen. The Scout troop meets on Wednesday evenings in a hut down by the river. The troop focuses its activities on water sports such as canoeing and sailing.

Elisabeth helps out at the local-authority youth club in her village. The club is open three nights a week and there are about fifty members who drop in from time to time. There are more boys than girls who use the club and ages range from thirteen to seventeen. Popular activities are five-a-side football and hanging out in the small coffee bar where there is a tape and CD player.

Both Jim and Elisabeth are involved in youthwork on a voluntary basis, but the kind of youthwork that they actually do is very different. A Scout troop is a different animal from a youth club, as anyone who has done both will tell you!

There are so many different approaches to youthwork. The sheer variety of youth-related activities can be bewildering. As a volunteer working with young people it is important that you are sure that your youthwork is useful and effective. Your time is a very valuable resource and you need to feel confident that what you are doing is worthwhile. This chapter aims to help you to step back from the youthwork you are currently involved with so that you can:

◆ analyse the youthwork you are doing

◆ evaluate your own youthwork

◆ make a choice about what kind of youthwork you want to do.

In this section we concentrate on analysing your youthwork. To do this I introduce the idea of 'youthwork models'. A model is a simple pattern of analysis. This pattern can be used to sum up in a quick and easy fashion how a particular approach to youthwork operates.

WHAT IS A MODEL?

A model is a picture of how a particular type of youthwork operates. So the Scouting model is a summary of how Scout troops work in general. The youth club model is similarly a summary of how youth clubs work. The point about models is that they help us to look at what we are doing more clearly. An architect will often summarize his or her plans by making a scale model of a building project. This model will help other

people to visualize quickly what the building will look like and they can assess, for instance, the effect of the project on the environment, or on nearby buildings. If you wanted to compare two different plans for the same building project, one of the easiest ways to do this would be to put two architect's models side by side.

Youthwork models work just like those made by architects—they help us to see quickly what is going on in one particular style of youthwork. Of course a youthwork model is not expressed as a three-dimensional plastic construction with little bits of moss that look like trees. When we talk about youthwork as models, we have to use words and ideas.

A youthwork model is a simple analysis of a particular approach to youthwork. There are three questions which get to the root of youthwork and you can use these to analyse any youthwork project. These questions are:

◆ **Aims:** What is the group trying to achieve?

◆ **Strategy:** How are the aims put into practice?

◆ **Client group:** What kinds of young people are catered for by this youthwork?

Types of youthwork vary greatly, but you can use these questions to sum them up. The final result of your analysis is a model. Using these models you are able very quickly to get a grasp of how a particular approach to youthwork operates. It is also possible to start to make comparisons between different ways of working with young people. The next section deals with how to evaluate different youthwork models in more depth, but, finally in this section, here are some examples of different types of youthwork. Each of these different approaches to work with young people can be expressed as a model. They each have **aims**, **strategy** and **client group**.

- ◆ **Detached youthwork:** Working on the streets or in a shopping centre, building friendships with young people.

- ◆ **Sports coaching:** Helping to run a team or other sporting activity.

- ◆ **Drop-in centre:** A place where young people can come for advice, support or just a warm place to be.

- ◆ **Youth fellowship:** A Christian nurture group focused on Bible study and prayer.

- ◆ **Youth empowerment groups:** Self-help groups which focus on particular issues affecting young people (for example, provision of accommodation for homeless young people).

I have taken one approach to youthwork—'The alcohol-free bar'—and expressed it as a model.

ALCOHOL-FREE BAR

(as compiled by The Dog and Biscuit management committee, see following section)

Aims:

- ◆ To provide a safe leisure environment for young people below the age of eighteen.

- ◆ To show a positive Christian response to the problem of drunkenness amongst local teenagers.

- ◆ To give a low-key Christian witness to local young people.

Strategy:

- ◆ Convert church hall into a bar-like venue.

- ◆ Advertise in local schools and on the streets the existence of the bar.

- ◆ Provide a number of youthworkers who can be a low-key Christian presence in the bar welcoming people and providing advice where appropriate.

- ◆ Run the occasional Christian event in the bar (for example, Christian rock band).

Client group:

- ◆ Young people who currently hang around in the town centre drinking illegally on the streets.

EXERCISE

1   Make a short list of different types of youthwork you can identify in your local area.

2   Take about forty minutes and analyse the youthwork you are currently involved in as a model by using the categories listed in this section: aims, strategy and client group.

FEEDBACK

1   In most towns there will probably be three or four different types of youthwork operating. Even connected with one church there may be a variety of different youthwork happening. These could include a youth fellowship, a Scout troop or Guide company. In some churches the most

significant youthwork that takes place happens in the church choir. You might have missed one or two important pieces of work with young people that happen in your local area such as the church choir because you did not recognize that this was in fact youthwork. It is worth thinking a bit more widely about what happens with and for young people in your local area over the next few weeks and adding any projects that you come across to your list.

2   When you have expressed your own youthwork situation as a model in terms of **aims**, **strategy** and **client group**, check your work against the example I have provided to see if you have covered similar or different areas. One important thing to bear in mind is that a model will always be a bit unreal. There are two main reasons for this:

(a) A model is a simplification. To express everything that happens in a group is impossible. The point of a model is that you can see clearly what is going on in that particular piece of youthwork. When you are looking at your model of youthwork it is always important to bear this fact in mind. The model helps us to see clearly *because* it is a simplification, but for that very reason it will be limited.

(b) A model is a generalization. Each model is a summary of characteristics which similar kinds of youthwork projects share. For instance most youth clubs will centre on games, but some might be more discussion based. It is good to bear in mind the fact that individual youthwork projects will differ in many ways from the generalized model.

EVALUATING YOUTHWORK USING MODELS

INSTRUCTIONS

This section takes the form of a case study. You are on the management committee of The Dog and Biscuit, an alcohol-free bar which has now been open for two years in 'Newtown'. The management committee are conducting an annual review of the work of the bar. The committee has asked David Kemp from PYT (Pioneer Youth Trust), a Christian youthwork organization, to write a report on the work. This report will form the basis of the review.

EXERCISE

You are reading through David Kemp's report a couple of days before the meeting. Your task is to read the report and then formulate an action plan to deal with the points raised. This plan should be written down in note form.

REPORT TO THE DOG AND BISCUIT MANAGEMENT COMMITTEE

From David Kemp, Area Supervisor for PYT

At the meeting of the management committee on 20 November we finalized our discussion on which 'model' of youthwork was operating at The Dog and Biscuit. We summarized this model under the headings 'Aims', 'Strategy' and 'Client Groups' (for the full text see previous section).

In preparing this report I have tried to refer back to the agreed model as a reference point for my evaluation of the work of the bar.

The alcohol-free bar model states that the main client group expected to use the facilities are 'young people who currently hang around in the town centre drinking illegally on the streets'.

The Dog and Biscuit in Newtown was set up by the local churches and it has been operating for two years. The aim of the project, as stated in the model, was that the client group should be those young people who were too young to get into the pubs but were still hanging around the town centre at night.

The bar is indeed a well-constructed facility with a genuine bar-like atmosphere. The facility is well staffed by one full-time co-ordinator and a team of fifteen volunteer youth-workers from the local churches. In preparing this report I conducted two surveys. The first was amongst those young people using the bar during the month of December. The second, conducted in the same month, was amongst young people on the streets in Newtown. These surveys threw up two main points.

* The majority of young people using the bar during this period were from the local churches. They saw the bar as a safe place in the centre of the town where they could meet up with their friends. A number of them mentioned the fact that their parents, who generally didn't like them to go into town at night, were happy if they went to the bar because it was run by the churches. It was clear that the young people, and their parents, felt a sense of ownership of the bar.

* The young people on the streets I spoke to said that they did not like going to the bar. Many of them said that they felt that the bar was too religious. They felt that when they went to the bar they were under pressure to become Christians. It wasn't the youthworkers at the bar they complained about: it was the young people who went to the local churches who made them feel uncomfortable. Some said that they felt unwelcome there because they did not go to church.

These two points raise three questions in my mind that the management committee need to wrestle with.

1. What do the churches really want to do - run an alcohol-free bar or help local young people on the streets? This is a question about the aims of the project. The stated aims might well be to reach local young people who are drinking on the streets. However, when The Dog and Biscuit proves to be unsuccessful in doing this, the churches need to ask themselves whether they are more committed to the idea of an alcohol-free bar than they are to the needs of young people in the local area.

2. The churches are probably very clear that their first aim is to reach the young people on the streets. However the lack of success of The Dog and Biscuit is a problem. The churches have invested a significant amount of money and time into this project and the launch was very high profile. A great deal of research went into the plans, including a visit to a similar project in London which appeared to be very succesful. Could it be that in Newtown this idea doesn't work? This is a question about 'Strategy'.

3. Is the problem the model or is it the way we have been putting the model into practice?

David Kemp 20.12.93

EEDBACK

David Kemp's report is very critical of the work of the bar and it raises a number of important questions. It is worth checking the notes you have made to make sure that you are well prepared for the meeting at which the management committee will discuss the future of The Dog and Biscuit. Here are some points which I have thought of to help you fine-tune your notes.

◆ Have you decided on the aims of the bar? Do you still hold to the view expressed in the original model that the primary aim of the bar is to reach young people on the streets?

◆ Have you considered that the whole idea of an alcohol-free bar might not work in Newtown?

◆ Is there some way that the culture in the bar created by the Christian young people could be moderated to make The Dog and Biscuit more welcoming to young people from outside the church?

Check your notes to make sure that you have at least expressed an opinion on these three points. Then carry on with the case study. The next paragraph is a summary of what happened at the meeting. Who do you most identify with—The Revd Smith, Mrs Beckett or Sam White?

AT THE MEETING

The management committee of The Dog and Biscuit met in January 1994 to discuss David Kemp's report. Here are the main points raised, taken from the minutes of the meeting.

The Revd Frank Smith: 'It seems clear that the bar is not reaching the young people we hoped it would. We should therefore reassess whether this is a project the churches should continue to back. Our church invested money in this project to help the young people on the streets. If the bar is judged to be a mistake we should sell the premises and use the money for the young people it was intended for.'

Jenny Beckett: 'The bar might not be helping the young people we first had in mind, but my daughter and the rest of St James's youth group go there every week. My husband and I, along with a good many parents in our church, covenant money to keep the project up and running. I think it is very valuable as it is and we should rejoice that our young people have somewhere safe to go on Saturday nights.'

Sam White: 'Our first priority should be outreach. We need to find ways of helping the Christian young people to be more welcoming. After all we are first and foremost called to be witnesses for Christ.'

THE DECISION

The group decided to work with the Christian young people to help them to be more evangelistically minded. It was decided to run a course on personal witness on Friday nights at the bar for regular members.

WHAT HAPPENED

Twelve months later David Kemp called in at the bar to see how things were going along. He found that, despite the personal witness course, the young people on the streets had never really found their way into the bar.

**XERCISE**

You meet David Kemp a few weeks after he visited The Dog and Biscuit, and he tells you what he has found. During the last year you have ceased to be a member of the committee due to the birth of a daughter. You decide however that you should let your feelings on this important matter be known.

In your notebook write a short letter referring to the original model and suggesting what should happen.

■ THE NUCLEUS MODEL

NPUT

As discussions at the management committee of The Dog and Biscuit might seem to prove, Christian youthwork is often pulled between two different client groups: Christian young people and young people in the wider community. The church has tended to solve this tension by adopting different patterns of youthwork which are specifically targetted at these two client groups. This section deals with the main approach that has been used to work with young people within the church. The following section ('A relational model of youthwork') looks at one way to reach out to those in the community.

For Christian young people, churches have evolved what I would call the nucleus model. This approach goes by a number of different names such as 'the youth fellowship', 'CYFA', 'the youth group' or 'the school CU'. In all of these cases the basic principles upon which this model works are essentially the same.

The nucleus model first came to popularity in the 1930s and 1940s. Churches began to realize that young people above the age of fourteen who had left Sunday school needed a separate meeting to help encourage them in the faith. These groups were primarily for 'insiders'. The children of churchgoers were to be brought together for fellowship. This 'youth fellowship' would involve teaching about the faith, worship and some form of recreation or social activity. Having established the 'nucleus' or core group of committed young people, the group could begin to reach out to non-Christian young people.

Since the 1930s this youth fellowship model of work has become the basic pattern for church-based youthwork adopted by evangelical churches in Britain. Organizations such as the Church Youth Fellowships Association and Scripture Union in schools are dedicated to encouraging the growth of these kinds of groups. In some churches this model of youthwork is the only one which operates. So popular is the nucleus model that it has come to be regarded as almost identical with Christian youthwork. For most churches, Christian youthwork equals running a nucleus model of youthwork.

The nucleus model

THE NUCLEUS MODEL

This model of youthwork has two main **aims**:

◆ to nurture young people in the Christian faith

◆ to share the message of Christ to those outside the group.

The **strategy** of the youth fellowship is best expressed in the phrase, 'The best people to evangelize young people are young people themselves.' This strategy is carried out by:

◆ gathering together a group of young people who are already affiliated with the church

◆ nurturing this group in the faith

◆ encouraging the group to bring their non-Christian friends along to the group or to special evangelistic events (for example, a Christian coffee bar or Christian

concert). The non-Christian friends are described as the 'fringe group'.

The **client group** is the children of churchgoing parents and their friends.

XERCISE

You need to allow at least one hour for this exercise.
  It is the beginning of a new year at the local technical college. Jane Simmonds joins the lunch queue behind Jeff, a friend from church. 'There's no notice to say when and where the Christian Union meets,' says Jane. 'That's because it folded in my first year,' says Jeff.

You go to the local church and Jane is in the youth group. At the end of the Sunday morning service Jane grabs you at the back of the church and asks if she can come and see you for some advice on setting up a CU.

Your task is to prepare what you are going to say to Jane based on the 'nucleus model'. Write down how you would explain this approach to Jane, using nucleus model diagram (opposite) as a starting point. So Jane is clear about what you are suggesting, give her a plan of action—including what you think should happen at the first meeting.

 EEDBACK

The nucleus model of youthwork is based on getting a group of Christians together. You should have included some way that Jane went about doing this in your plan. A poster on the notice board may bring a few Christians out of the woodwork, but Jane would probably be more successful making a list of all the Christians she already knows at the technical college and then over a period of a week or two trying to get in touch with them to see if they would like to form a Christian Union.

You have probably thought about the aims of the nucleus model, but you should also think about how these aims should apply in the technical college. I would probably talk to Jane about the need for Christians in the college to meet together to pray and support each other.

The first stage in Jane's plan would have to include a way to get the Christians together to encourage each other to grow in the faith. Here's my outline plan for the first meeting:

1   Introductions: welcome to the CU by Jane.

2   Getting to know you: a brief time of sharing for everyone to say who they are, what course they are on at the college and a bit about their church background.

3   Bible passage: a reading talking about being together as God's people (for example, 1 Corinthians 12:12–27).

4   A brief discussion of the aims of the CU.

5   Prayer in small groups for each other.

NPUT

For those young people who already attend church, the nucleus model is extremely effective. Alongside this approach, churches have also adopted a number of different youthwork models to reach out to those in the community who don't attend church. The youth club is a well-known example of this. There was a time when the majority of churches would have tried to include in their weekly programme activities which were for both insiders and outsiders. David Watson, writing in the 1960s, set out a plan for church youthwork which catered for the needs of those both inside and outside the church (*Towards Tomorrow's Church*, Falcon, 1966).

The plan, which was put into action in the church where David was curate, involved running a church youth fellowship for young people who were committed Christians on a Sunday evening in the home of the youth leader, but there was also what was called an 'open youth club'. The open youth club happened in the church hall and it provided social activities for the Christian young people as well as being open to young people who did not attend the youth fellowship. The idea behind this club was that it gave the Christian young people an opportunity to witness to the non-Christian young people who came along.

This basic pattern was much copied around the country and it had the merit of being a unified pattern of youthwork which attempted to cater for young people from a variety of backgrounds. Thirty years later most churches have dropped the 'open youth club' idea. There are many reasons for this, not least the fact that young people in the 1990s seem to be less attracted to a youth club programme. There is also the fact that local-authority youth clubs are on the whole much better equipped (for example, with decent sports facilities). Alongside this is the realization that the open youth club has not been an easy place to share the Christian faith with young people. Young people in the 1960s may well have moved from the youth club to join the youth fellowship, but this movement, envisaged by David Watson, has dried up in the last decade.

The loss of the open youth club as a viable method of outreach has left many churches with a vacuum in their approach to young people from outside the culture and social setting of the church. If we look around the churches today we have to admit that there are comparatively few places where there is a genuine attempt to reach out to young people who don't easily fit into the youth-fellowship-type approach. For a while in the 1980s we attempted to counter this lack of outreach by running events such as rock concerts. These have in some places been very successful. However, increasingly we have realized that these kinds of events work best as a supplement to the nucleus model. The rock-concert-type event works well as an occasion for young people in the youth fellowship to bring their friends along to the church. It has not, however, solved the problem of outreach beyond these friendship networks. The nucleus model is limited by the ability of Christian young people to build friendships across cultural or racial barriers.

EXERCISE

Write a brief answer to the following question:

In your local area, how successful is the nucleus model in reaching out to young people who don't fit the social make-up of the church?

A RELATIONAL MODEL OF YOUTHWORK

INPUT

People often find the relational model difficult to grasp. One of the reasons for this is that relationships are less easily observed. A youth club is a building, a sports team has regular meetings, but relationships are much less easy to pin down. It is worth remembering that this approach to youthwork has no gimmicks, no programmes, no buildings. Imagine two people meeting up, sharing interests and doing things together. Over a period of time they become friends. This in short is the relational approach to youthwork.

EXERCISE

The relational model starts by asking where young people naturally hang out in the local community. This could be the local shopping centre, the youth club, a sports centre or the local school.

Take about fifteen minutes to brainstorm where you think young people spend their time in your local area.

FEEDBACK

You may have found this last exercise a little difficult. It is not normal for adults to enquire where young people hang out. You may have found that you had very little clue where young people get together in your town, city or village. If this is the case, it might be a good idea to do a little research. This doesn't have to be too difficult. At its most basic, you could start by keeping your eyes skinned for young people next time you go out in the evening or at the weekend. You could also ask the young people you already know where young people gather.

INPUT

THE RELATIONAL APPROACH

Knowing where young people get together is one thing. The question is: 'How do you start to do youthwork with these young people?' The relational approach to youthwork is specifically designed to reach out to young people who are outside the present social and cultural world of the church. This is the approach to youthwork which was pioneered by Oxford Youth Works and it forms the background to the rest of this workbook.

In the middle of the 1980s a group of people in Oxford recognized that there was a need to try to develop a new way to reach out to young people who did not currently have any contact with the church. The result was what we have called at Oxford Youth Works 'the relational model of youthwork'. This model is based on four very simple principles:

◆ Christian adults meeting young people where the young people themselves hang out and feel comfortable

◆ Christian adults forming supporting friendships based on the interests and activities of the young people

◆ Christian adults taking the time to share the message about Jesus in terms and ways that make sense within the cultural world of the young people

◆ young people who have heard the message of Jesus and responded to him starting to form their own worship.

I have already described this approach in some depth in two books. The first, *Youth Culture and the Gospel* (HarperCollins, 1992), deals with how we make relationships with young people and how we can share the faith with them in ways they can easily relate to. The second, *Worship and Youth Culture* (HarperCollins, 1993), describes the setting up of an alternative worship service for young people. In the rest of this section I will give a brief summary of how the relational model works in practice, but I want to refer you to these other books because they deal with the material in much more depth.

EXERCISE

Central to the relational approach to youthwork is a belief that the ministry of Jesus was based on forming relationships with people. Read the first three chapters of Mark's Gospel and take about thirty minutes to note the kinds of relationships you think Jesus formed with people. Here are my observations to use as a guideline:

In Mark 1–3 we see Jesus making a great many relational approaches to people.

Here are some of the things I noticed in chapter 1 which you can use to compare with the kinds of things you have put on your own list.

1:9 Jesus was baptized. This means he was willing to identify with people as they came to John for cleansing from sin. A symbolic identification is happening here.

1:17 'Come with me,' Jesus told the disciples. Jesus had partners in his ministry who learned about the work as it happened.

1:29 Jesus maintained relationships with the synagogue. He was not a complete religious loner by any means.

1:38 Preaching was important in Jesus's ministry, but he took a group with him.

1:41 Jesus felt deeply about the people he ministered to. He was not a detached, professional healer. He was affected by the suffering that he saw around him.

FEEDBACK

I am convinced that we should try to base our youthwork on the example of Jesus. I realize that we are not divine. But we are called to be witnesses to him in the way we live. The relational approach to youthwork notes how Jesus was extremely personal in his dealings with people; he identified with them and met them where their need was greatest.

Take about fifteen minutes to answer the following question:

If you were to adopt a relational approach to youthwork in your local area, what would you have to change in the youthwork you are currently doing?

Here is a brief summary of how the relational approach is applied by Oxford Youth Works.

1   **Contact:** First we find ways of meeting young people on their own territory. This could be a local estate, an ice rink or a shopping centre. Our favourite approach has been to volunteer to help out in local schools in games lessons or art periods, or just to be around the school campus chatting to young people. Building up a relationship with the local school has taken some time, but in general we have been welcomed by those we have approached, especially where we can work closely with a Christian member of staff who can supervise what we do. Chapter 2 will deal with meeting young people for the first time, but in short we just start to get to know the young people wherever we meet them. To do this you need to be able to meet them at least twice a week.

2   **Extended contact:** We have found that through hanging out in the right places we get to meet a group of young people. This can happen surprisingly quickly. Friendships with different groups will

progress in different ways. But, for instance in my own work with young lads who play in rock bands, I have found that through our shared interests we naturally find other things, outside of the school setting, which we can do—for example, going to concerts, watching videos or playing together in the bands. With other groups of young people, friendship can grow just by going shopping together or going to the ice rink or swimming baths—anything which will help you to enjoy yourselves and to get to know each other better. In some situations we have taken groups away overnight to a youth centre.

3   **Sharing Jesus:** After about a year or two of getting to know each other we often want to share a bit more about the Christian side of our lives. We have used discussion groups for this, or in some cases we have invited young people to a Christian event. The best way in our experience, however, is to run a holiday where we can talk a bit about Jesus in a simple way. Of course the friendships we have developed with the young people will in themselves be a powerful witness to the gospel. They show that God is interested in them and that he cares. Talking about Jesus, however, makes this caring more concrete, it shows where we are coming from and what makes us care.

4   **Learning about Jesus:** After our holiday away some of the young people decide that the Christian faith is worth exploring. We hold a short and simple worship time for these young people which includes an introduction to prayer, worship and fellowship as well as some more teaching about the Christian life. We focus on helping the young people to get to grips with the Bible and the Christian faith for themselves. We want them to use their own words to describe their experience because

this means that they are making the faith
their own (for more on this see chapter 8).

5   **Alternative worship:** This is a service
in a local church run by some of the young
people who have come to faith through the
work of Oxford Youth Works. The service
uses songs they have written and words that
they have thought about together. The
service is planned by the young people and
it is a place where they can start to build
their own Christian fellowship.

INTERPERSONAL SKILLS FOR YOUTHWORKERS

 2

J u d e   L e v e r m o r e

INTRODUCTION

Communicating with young people can be the most rewarding experience. Rarely do you feel as a youthworker that you've actually got through, made contact with them, touched base. You know, that feeling when you see in their eyes that they know what you're on about, and more than that, that they care about what you're on about. It takes a long time and a fair amount of work to get to that stage, but believe me, it's worth it!

THE COMMUNICATION PROCESS

INPUT

Communication is more about practice than it is about theory. It is about getting involved with others. It is the sending of thoughts, feelings, attitudes and knowledge, as well as ideas, in such a way that another person can receive them for themselves. It is about 'making things common' between people. It is also a process that promotes change in individuals and in society. *It is vital!*

INTERACTION

On the following page is a long list of words and ideas about the topic of communication. In your notebook pick out twenty that you think are the most important. When you have chosen your twenty, try to link them together in groups of related ideas. For example, you may think that newspapers and TV link with the word 'media'; if so then put a circle around them in a colour, then circle others that link in different colours. When you have finished you will need to do a key of all the different colours and what they mean.

NEWSPAPERS TV RADIO whine

musical instruments posture eyes body language

corrections BLANK WRITING

NOISES feedback filed fax

perceptions stutter ideas STYLE FORMAT

crowds discussion observation natter

soul links art CODES

sharing SHOUTS NON-VERBAL games voice telephone

niggle

chatter caring intuition twitter groups

empathy CRYING

flirt ASSERTIVE negative answers MUSIC

tuning in smile attitude Grunts

tone tension

films yelling facial expression

clothing PHRASING honesty programming

vacant MUMBLING attention text actions

video touch gossip

words listening SIGNAL advertising magazines

semaphore SPEECH laughter QUESTIONS conversation

EEDBACK

Communication is a very complex thing and it has so many aspects. I expect you found it hard to pick just twenty and to choose which ones to leave out. Did you naturally pick words that linked? I find that making the links is what is really difficult because so many different ways of linking come to mind once you start to think about it. For example 'body language' is a form of 'non-verbal communication', so they can be linked together. However it also appears whenever there is an image of a human being, so links can be made with TV and art and photography as well as with other aspects of non-verbal communication, like crying or silence or drum beats.

Do many of your links overlap? If not, is it because you chose things that fitted nicely into groups or is it that you need to think more about how aspects of communication fit together?

This chapter is about interpersonal skills—that is communicating with one other person face to face, on a one-to-one basis. It's the form of interaction that most of us use most of the time and yet the one most of us think about and analyse the least. How many of your words relate to that aspect of the vast subject of communication? It may be not very many. That's OK. I find that most people tend to think in terms of media, sermons and telling people things when they think about communication—especially when they think about communicating the gospel—when really communication is a process that human beings undertake to share feelings, ideas and concepts, even those as big as God.

HOW COMMUNICATION WORKS—
THE THEORY

Communication is a meeting of meanings—at least that's the idea. Theory is all very well, and it helps us to understand reality but what does it have to offer the average person who just wants to do a bit of youthwork just a bit better than they're doing it at present? Well any communication from one person to another may have distortions in it, but a communication from one person in one sub-culture (youth) to another (adult) is bound to be subject to even more problems. So how can theory help? I suppose it can help by giving us a framework, by showing us in stages how communication is supposed to happen by highlighting the pitfalls and problems. All this gives us a picture of what might be happening in our dealings with young people, and that means that we might be able to look at it, see where we've gone wrong in the past and work on ways of doing it better next time. So here goes, back to the theory.

Communication is a meeting of meanings, but how does this happen? All communication comes to us in the form of codes. These codes may include some of the words that you chose from the list earlier.

Codes can be *words*.

Codes can be *signs*.

Codes can be *images*.

Just thinking about something you want to communicate will not get the message across, unless you're into thought transference or playing a role in *Star Trek— The Movie*! Messages need to be put into code. We all do it without even thinking about it. The theory goes like this:

The person who wants to send the message (called the 'transmitter'), has to encode their message before they send it.

'That's a nice jumper Pete is wearing.'

The person who is the recipient of this piece of communication (called the 'receiver'), then has to receive this message and then decode it before they can understand it.

Let's look at it in terms of a specific example.

Bob, our 'transmitter', thinks, 'That's a nice jumper Pete is wearing.' So he puts the message into code, in this case the English language, and he says out loud, 'That's a nice jumper you are wearing.'

Pete hears the speech and, as he understands English, he can decode it and so he thinks, 'Oh, Bob likes my jumper.'

Seems simple enough! However like all things in life there are complications! The major complication in the process of communication is distortion.

Distortion can be physical.

Something physically stops the message getting through

Distortion can be psychological.

Something in our heads stops the message getting through.

It can happen where the message is sent

where it is being received

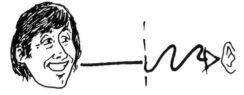

and where it is decoded.

So then, if the message is distorted while it is being sent, the receiver might not get the codes or might only get some of them. Maybe Bob mumbles or the background music is too loud, or maybe Pete is hard of hearing or becomes distracted. If any of those happen, Pete may never know that Bob likes his jumper.

If the message is distorted as Pete decodes it, it may become altered in his perception. Or again it may be incomplete, or totally absent. So many times in conversation we are misunderstood, but when you think of all the possibilities, it's not so surprising.

Distortion can also happen because of what's going on inside us. For example, if Pete is convinced that Bob doesn't like him the conversation might go like this:

Bob: That's a nice jumper you're wearing.
Pete: There's no need to be sarcastic. I like it.
Bob: Well I was only trying to be friendly.
Pete: Oh, sure. Look, just push off!

Oh dear! This is distortion!

So that's the theory. Codes are what matter in communication, the question now is: 'How do we use this theory to help us in our youthwork?' The first thing to think about is what codes young people use and whether they are the same as ours. Different age groups have their own codes, verbal and non-verbal. A lady of eighty would be happy to say that she went to a party that was quite 'gay'; a girl of eighteen would not. The word 'gay' has changed in its meaning between generations. Different social class groups, different areas of the country and different ethnic groups all use different codes. Men have different codes from women. It is likely that we are going to be in a different category, in at least one of these, to the young person with whom we are trying to communicate. We are likely to be a different age, different social class, have different friends and be of a different religious or spiritual persuasion. How on earth are we ever going to communicate? Of course the answer is that we have to learn a different set of codes, a different language.

In youthwork terms maybe the biggest communication distortion happens when the transmitter's code means something different in the receiver's culture and vice versa.

If the transmitter is a young person and they are speaking in a language we don't understand, communication is bound to be difficult! Not only that but it's important to remember that codes are not only what we say; we communicate in our image, our clothes and our body language too. A one-finger salute that may seem offensive to you or me may be a form of greeting to a young person. Misunderstanding and misinterpretation between adults and young people are almost inevitable. If we are to be friends of young people, to listen to them, hear what they say and discover where they are coming from, and if we are to be heard by them, then we need to study and to learn their language—verbal and non-verbal.

EXERCISE

Think about one of the young people that you know. Do they have any codes that they use that are different from ones you use? Do they use words that are foreign to you, or dress in a way that is saying something to the adult world? Spend some time thinking about this now. When you have this young person clearly in your mind, write a description of them in your notebook. Concentrate on their appearance and language, and any codes you have noticed. For example, they might say, 'That party was wicked,' meaning, 'That party was great.' Whereas you or I might say, 'I really had a good time at that party.' Take about half an hour to do this; make it as detailed and in depth as you can.

How do you think you might go about further research into the codes of young people in your area? Write some suggestions in your book. Spend another half an hour on this.

Finally for this section—does the example of the misunderstanding between Pete and Bob over the jumper ring any bells with you? Can you think of a time when you have misinterpreted someone or been misinterpreted because of distortion? Copy an empty version of the following form into your notebook and spend one more half hour filling it in.

Example of misinterpretation.	How I felt about this.

FEEDBACK

One way I learn about the current codes is by watching and listening to young people. If I sit myself down on a bench in the park with my sandwiches one lunchtime, near a group of young people, I can watch them unobserved. It's a bit like being an undercover agent!

If I did this what might I see? Well, young people in my area currently use lots of touching of hair to communicate affection; the girls and lads plait each others hair, braid it, stroke it, put beads in it and so on. When they wouldn't touch any other part of that person's body, they use hair as a first point of bodily contact, rather like people used to shake hands!

What might this mean then if a young man touches my hair, or offers to plait or bead it? Well I suppose it means acceptance of me, not as an adult but as a friend. As far as language is concerned one of the words around now that young people I know use is 'kicking', meaning really good.

Observation is important because some of the codes that young people use, they use without being aware of them. So if you ask them what a certain behaviour meant the reply you would get would be likely to be, 'Dunno mate.'

Eventually, however, you will have to ask if you want to know about language codes. A fairly useful way of doing this is to devise a questionnaire. This has the added advantage of giving you an excuse to go up to a group and talk to them. However, from my point of view, by far the best way is to talk informally with a group that you already know, in a low-key way, when something happens or is said that you don't understand.

The codes of young people, their own particular words, phrases, ways of dressing and so on, vary considerably from town to town—even, in my experience, from school to school and friendship group to friendship group. It is one of the challenges for the youthworker to keep in touch with what's going on 'on the street' so to speak. Things change constantly, so much so that it's impossible to keep up, but that's part of the reason for the codes. Young people need a language of their own, one that adults can't penetrate. They are developing a sense of identity, a sense of themselves as part of a group that is different to other groups, and very different to the world of the adult. I feel that it's important to allow them this, it's important for me not to become an expert on their codes but to allow them to teach me what they mean. They are the experts in this field because they made up the codes (although they might not be aware of it, or see their way of communicating in these terms), they know what's what and we are just students of it, we must be honest.

Do you feel that if I read your description I could draw a picture of the young person you described and be fairly accurate about it? Re-read your description in the light of someone wanting to draw them. Have you missed out any vital bits of information, or have you omitted only unimportant things? Maybe the young person you chose to describe uses more language codes than visual ones and so your description is more about what they say than how they look. If this is so, a drawing of them won't be

possible and that's OK. However it is important to look in a balanced way at the young people we're describing. If you have written your description only in terms of language, or written it only in terms of clothes and gestures, you may have been presenting an unbalanced view. Young people communicate in visual and verbal ways and you need to be aware of both. In describing your young person and the codes they use, you have begun to think in depth about them in a way that you may not have done before. This will help you in your understanding not just of the content of their communication but also of the meanings they attach to it. Well done!

The final part of the exercise was about misunderstandings. I can remember many occasions when what I've said has been misinterpreted. Often this is a result of my sarcasm. It is called the 'lowest form of wit' and it seems to me that many people in our culture overuse it. This seems especially so of adults to young people. It is easy to use sarcasm as a means of control, using it to keep unruly teenagers at arms length, in their place, to stop them giving us too much lip and getting out of control. Is this your experience? When you filled out your form, what did you find was the cause of your misinterpretation? Was it something physical, like noise, or something emotional, like an assumption that the other person didn't like you? On doing this exercise before, I have found that where the misinterpretation is physical, the feelings accompanying it are less negative than if the cause of misinterpretation is emotional. This highlights the fact that our ability to communicate is tied up with our emotions, probably more than we realize. When misinterpretation occurs, we feel bad about it; sometimes that bad feeling can make the situation worse, compounding the problem that was there in the first place. Young people are often on the receiving end of misinterpretation and they are misunderstood most often because of the codes that they use. We don't often consider how they feel about these misunderstandings. Now you have thought about your feelings, do you feel any more sympathetic to young people who say, 'No one understands me'?

So then, that's the theory of how communication works. In this section you have covered the way communication is encoded, sent and received, looked at how distortion can occur and begun to think about how emotions tie in with all this. The next section will look at putting this theory into practise, and getting you actually talking to a young person (about time)!

GETTING STARTED—A LOOK AT BASIC BODY LANGUAGE

INSTRUCTIONS

For this section to be completed you will need to get together some equipment. You'll need a mirror, full length if possible, in a quiet place, where you can make faces in it without an audience to put you off.

NPUT

Before even opening our mouths we communicate with people in whose presence we are. Just being with a young person, we cannot help but communicate to them messages in code about ourselves. One of the ways we communicate these codes is in body language. As you learned from the previous section, we communicate in what we wear, how we stand, our body and facial expression and all this before saying a word. Body language says a lot—there are books and books written about the subject—but what follows are some basics that it is helpful to know.

YOUR HEIGHT

How high you are and the height of the person you are talking to are said to be an indicator of the status you feel you have in the relationship.

If you are higher than the person you are talking to you are likely to be seen as superior, and if you are lower you are likely to be seen as inferior.

This theory is helpful for us as youthworkers to know. When you're talking to young people who are used to feeling inferior to adults it is good to reverse the process. This means getting lower than the young person you are talking to. Easy to do if you're short like me, but harder if you're six foot. Basically it means if they're standing you sit, if they sit in a chair then you sit on the floor and so on. It can mean that you end up sitting in the gutter but that's good for our adult egos.

Being at the same or lower level to someone communicates, 'I want to be your friend', 'I don't want to be in authority over you'. Conversely, if you want to give instructions for a game or something where you need to be in charge then get everyone to sit down and you stand or, if they stand, then you stand on a chair!

YOUR BODY

A closed body means, 'Go away I don't want to talk.' So open your arms don't cross them, pull back your shoulders don't hunch, don't cross your legs tightly. Your aim should be to sit, stand or walk freely and easily.

YOUR FACE

Smile, just slightly and relax. You can practise this later in front of a mirror. Put on a 'welcome please talk to me' face. Try looking in a mirror and saying, 'Hello, I really do want to talk to you' in your head while you smile slightly. Your face should look softer than if you just smile and nod a greeting. Next time you are cleaning your teeth, brushing your hair or whatever in front of a mirror, have a go.

YOUR EYES

It is important to look at someone when you talk to them—we all know how disconcerting it can be to talk to someone who doesn't look at you. It can make people look untrustworthy. Staring, on the other hand, can be just as off-putting. It's necessary to know that looking away from people may give them the message that you're not interested, or haven't the time for them. If you can look at them, quickly look away and then look back, you should be saying in body-language terms, 'I want to hear what you say.'

YOUR POSITION

Being too close, or too far away, can prevent a young person talking to you. They can feel either that you are disinterested, or that you are a frightening and intimidating person that they just wish they could escape from. Neither of these two are a good place from which to start explaining the good news of Jesus!

So then, there are some body language basics. Now it's time to have a go.

EXERCISE

Spend some time now in front of your mirror. Get yourself comfortable in a chair so that you can see yourself without straining. Try sitting in a way that communicates openness and a willingness to talk, a way that says, 'I'm friendly.' How does it look?

Now sit in a way that says, 'Go away, I'm not interested.' How does that look? Get up and go out of the room. When you come back in, sit down in front of the mirror in your usual way. Overall do you look more or less friendly when you sit in your usual way? If you look on balance less friendly, what do you need to do to your body language to look more interested and open? Make a note now, in your book, of changes you need to make. If you already look fairly approachable, are there any improvements that could be made? Write these down in your notebook.

**I need to _____
to be more friendly looking, and generally more cuddly to a young person.**

FEEDBACK

On the whole, most people look quite relaxed and approachable in their normal pose. However, when we get nervous or upset our body language tends to become more closed. Talking to young people can be a nerve-racking experience, so it is worth practising this open body language so that when you're in a situation with a young person and you feel a bit up-tight you can consciously adopt a body position you know looks relaxed and friendly, even if you feel quite the opposite.

You may have felt that the exercise was too false to enter into fully, too unreal to be of benefit. I think this is unlikely. It is always worth spending time reflecting on how others see us, on the messages and codes we send out without our knowing it. Do you have a long list of improvements? If you have, don't be too hard on yourself. This only goes to show that you will gain a lot from the practise. It also shows how good you are at observation. Accurate observation and reflection on your practice are two things that in my opinion characterize good youthworkers.

Body language is something that I believe it is possible to get too hung up about. You need to have a balance between good, open, friendly smiles, eye contact and body position, and being true to yourself and your character. Young people see through fraud more quickly than a hot knife moves through butter. I'm also a great believer in not trying too hard to read other people's body language, not trying to read things into the way they stand. The young people you come into contact with are still learning the codes, or may have developed codes of their own. You are doing no one any favours becoming a super-sleuth people watcher, who thinks they know what someone is thinking by the way they hold their pool cue! You are likely to be wrong, likely to upset or annoy them by your analysis and likely to have wasted a great deal of time and effort to reach that conclusion. So concentrate on the messages you are sending in the body language codes you use and make sure you are saying what you meant to say. Then young people may be willing to talk to you.

GETTING STARTED—THE 'HOW TO' OF BEGINNING A CONVERSATION WITH A YOUNG PERSON

INSTRUCTIONS

What follows is some theory of how to start a conversation. When you have read this, the exercise will ask you to have a go! So that you can practise in safety, you need to find a willing adult to practise on. It will take about half an hour of their time, so they need to be fairly tolerant. They also need to be the sort of person who can give you some feedback on how you did, so don't pick anyone you can't stand criticizing you. The ideal person would be the type of person you would choose to teach you to drive! You also need a quiet place to practise where you won't be interrupted and where you can both sit in comfort.

 NPUT

As you saw from the last section, body language is important in communication. All the same, it is no good at all if you don't eventually speak! Conversation is how relationships happen—there is little possibility of a deep friendship (or indeed any friendship) developing if no words are exchanged. So how do you start speaking? Is it just a question of saying the first thing that comes into your head? Well no. If you do that you could be heading for trouble.

Almost everyone uses one of three topics with which to start. In fact I can't think of anything else you could start with. These three are:

◆ the situation

◆ the other person

◆ yourself.

Let's look at each of these and I'll explain each in a bit more detail.

THE SITUATION

An example of this could be, 'It's cold in here, isn't it?' In other words, it is using the things around as the subject matter to start the ball rolling.

This means you have to use all your skills of observation to see something worth remarking on. It's about looking around and using what you see to construct an opening sentence.

THE OTHER PERSON

An example of this could be, 'I really like your boots.' To use this way of opening you must observe what the other person is doing, wearing or saying, and pick up on it.

You could use this topic whatever your situation. Unless you are talking to yourself you always have another person around when you start a conversation, so why not use that fact to your advantage?

YOURSELF

An example of this could be, 'I play football every Saturday.' It's a way of starting that is based on your perspective.

It's another one that you can always use, and it's often what people use when they're nervous because it's something that you can be sure of.

So there you have it—three topics with which to begin. Just as you thought you had that all understood, I'd like to introduce you to another three. Not three more topics, but three ways in which to introduce each topic. You see each topic can be launched into in one of three ways. You can:

◆ ask a question

◆ state a fact

◆ voice an opinion

about any one of the three topics. Below are some examples of each of these.

ASKING A QUESTION

'What's your name?'

'Do you come here often?'

'How do you join this club?'

STATING A FACT

'My name's Jude.'

'You came here last week.'

'You have to be a member to be in this club.'

VOICING AN OPINION

'I think you're called John.'

'I believe I saw you here last week.'

'It seems to me that most people in this club are members.'

So with three topics and three ways of starting, you have all you need to know in order to open a conversation. Of course it's not that easy in practice, and obviously some ways and some topics work better in different situations. But for now it's a start that will help you on your way.

EXERCISE

This is when you need your willing adult! Get yourself two chairs, preferably of the same type, or at least get yourselves seated at the same kind of height (you could both be sitting on the floor, or both on a desk). Now try out each topic as a way of starting a conversation and see how well the conversation goes.

For example, you could start by talking about the situation:

> You have to be a member to be in this club.

Let the chat between you be as natural as possible. If the conversation does start, let it go on for up to a minute. If it just dries up, don't worry, just stop. When you have finished each topic, ask your willing adult which they found the best. Which seemed the most natural and why? Record your results in your notebook.

Now repeat this exercise, but this time use each of the different ways: asking a question, voicing an opinion and stating a fact.

For example, asking a question about the situation:

> How do you join this club?

So all in all you will have started nine different conversations!

As before, ask your willing adult which was the best in their opinion, and record what they felt in your notebook.

Which of the nine ways was best for you? Do you and your friend agree? Can you come to an agreement as to what is generally the best way to start a conversation? After you have discussed it, complete the following sentence in your notebook:

In my opinion, in general, the best way to start a conversation with a young person is _____ .

EEDBACK

This exercise is a difficult one! It is very hard to start a conversation in a set way when you are used to hardly thinking about it. It is especially hard when you are trying it out on a friend who you know and are used to just chatting away to. Despite the fact that it is fairly unrealistic, this kind of trying things out before you do it for real can be invaluable as it helps you to eliminate glaring mistakes before you make them. For example, unless you are the world's most riveting person, then starting a conversation using yourself as the topic is a big no-no. Young people are not very interested in the adult world you inhabit. They have more important things to think about—like girlfriends, spots and how to persuade their parents to let them go to that gig on Saturday. However, how many times have you tried to start a conversation like this:

> **Hello, my name's John, I'm the new youthworker.**

In my experience this type of start is not likely to get a response, let alone produce much of a conversation, unless you have a very talkative teenager who happens to be feeling bored at the time.

Did you find that starting with yourself led to a dead end? If not, maybe your willing adult was being too polite! Most young people who you are trying to talk to for the first time owe you nothing, not even courtesy. They will not be generous! Talking about the situation can be a better bet. For a start, it's natural, it is unlikely to be threatening and, especially if you ask a question about it, you put them in the position of power. They become the expert and everyone likes to feel important in that way. Did you find this topic led to a longer chat? It may be that you didn't, due to a lack of inspiring surroundings:

> **These walls are very plain aren't they?**

The generally agreed theory is that starting with a question about the other person works best. So you can feel very pleased with yourself if that's the conclusion you came to! If you didn't, then remember that as every situation and every person is going to be different then there can be no 'right' answer as such. In your situation with that particular person another way was more natural.

Just a word from my own experience (bitter experience) about starting conversations with questions about the other person. Remember, we are talking about young people here. Young people when being talked to by adults tend to get defensive, so a question like, 'Do you always smoke Marlboro cigarettes?' can get an angry response. Not really the first impression you might be after.

One more thing—about names. Asking a young person their name isn't always a good idea as a starting point. To begin with you will probably be too stressed to remember it. Also it doesn't lead anywhere. In addition, names are something that give you the power, they don't know yours and you can use their name to call them, to tell them off and so on. It's a bit too 'teacher like', as a young person I know described it. So on the whole my advice would be to hold back on asking names until they know yours. You can usually discover names by listening in to conversations anyway, and if and when you do ask then it's good to phrase it like this: 'What do you like to be called?'

That gives them the opportunity to tell you their nickname or surname, or whatever they prefer, and it's very different to what they would be asked at school. It puts you in the realm of friends, which is your aim.

Anyway, enough pearls of wisdom from me! That is this section finished. Well done!

CONTINUING CONVERSATIONS— HOW TO CARRY ON ONCE YOU'VE GOT AN INITIAL REPLY

INSTRUCTIONS

For the exercise at the end of this section you will be asked to try something out in conversation with a young person. So if you need to arrange it so you can meet some young people while this section is still fresh in your mind, this would be a good time to do it.

INPUT

I like things in threes, and once again there are three things that can help you to keep young people talking once you've got their attention.

ENCOURAGING, NONCOMMITTAL RESPONSES

How we respond to young people greatly affects whether or not the conversation continues. These are wonderful little words and noises that get people to carry on talking:

◆ 'Right . . .'

◆ 'I see . . .'

◆ 'Hmmmmmm . . .'

◆ 'Interesting . . .'

◆ 'Tell me more . . .'

They depend on your tone of voice and they need to sound genuine, but most of us use them a lot of the time when we speak in conversation. Next time you are on the phone to a friend, listen to yourself and you will probably find you use all these at some point or other. These little words are code for 'please carry on talking, I'm interested'. That's why we use them more on the phone. On the phone you can't be seen and you therefore cannot convey the 'please go on' message through you body language so it needs to be verbal. They are a kind of verbal body language. Young people don't look at adults who talk to them very well. Our encouraging, open body language needs to be reinforced by these verbal responses. Some of us naturally use them more than others. If you tend to be the type who remains silent unless actually using words in sentences, you might want to try peppering your conversation with more of these helpful little sounds, and see if people stay and talk for longer. One more thing they do is convey an impression of you having plenty of time. Most adults have very little or no time for young people. Giving of your time will make you very valuable to them.

OPEN QUESTIONS

Closed questions close down the conversation. They are questions that force the person into a 'yes' or 'no' answer.

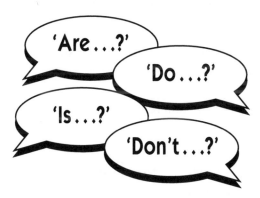

Open questions get the conversation going. They allow for the person to give a descriptive answer and let things develop.

Open questions start with:

◆ 'How . . .?'

◆ 'When . . .?'

◆ 'Where . . .?'

◆ 'What . . .?'

and sometimes

◆ 'Why . . .?'

Closed questions start with:

◆ 'Are . . .?'

◆ 'Do . . .?'

◆ 'Is . . .?'

◆ 'Don't . . .?'

FREE INFORMATION

This is the name given to little things that people say that give you clues about where to go next in the conversation. To use it effectively you need to listen carefully to things that are said that you didn't particularly ask. An example is in the illustration over the page:

Free information tends to be small facts, often about other people, but it can also be hidden (or not so hidden) emotion. We communicate not just in language, remember, so body language and non-verbal clues can also be free information.

XERCISE

This is where you need your young person. Next time you are in conversation with a young person try keeping the conversation going using an open question followed by lots of encouraging noncommittal responses. When you get home write an account of how it went. Record as much as you can remember of the conversation and write down how you felt about it. Did it feel natural or did you feel daft?

As a written exercise change the following questions from closed to open:

◆ Do you still feel upset about failing your exams?

◆ Would you like to talk about it?

◆ Is it difficult to get to youth group?

◆ Are you coping since your girlfriend dumped you?

EEDBACK

How did your conversation go? Did it dry up or did you manage to keep it going? Sometimes it is very hard to think about so many things at once. You were trying to think about what was being said, formulate an open question in your head, remember all the little noises and words to use and keep it all in your head so you could write it down. If the conversation was not the most natural in the world it is hardly surprising!

I think that learning to use open questions is the most helpful technique to have at your fingertips in talking with young people.

The change from, 'Did you go out last night?' to, 'What did you do last night?' can make all the difference in how quickly you can get to know young people. It also affects the quality of the information that you get back, giving you much more in the way of free information to go on. This allows you to form the next open question, and off you go—there'll be no stopping you!

GETTING DEEPER—A LOOK AT REALLY LISTENING

NPUT

Most of us don't really listen. We think we do, but in reality we are just spending the time while people are talking to us formulating our own replies. The sort of listening that is of value to young people needs to go deeper than that. It requires a giving of ourselves because it is hard work. It requires that we put aside our egos and concentrate on the other. It is actually about love. To really listen to someone is to love them.

So how do you do it? Well it might seem obvious but the first thing you need to do is to be quiet. Listening requires us not to talk. For extroverts, and most people in youthwork are, this is not as easy as it sounds. But keeping quiet is not enough. It is no good being silent if I am allowing my mind to daydream. The term given to the type of quiet that listens is *active listening*.

Once again there are three key parts to this:

EYE CONTACT

We've looked at this earlier, but remember, you must look at someone to show you listen.

ATTENTIVE BODY LANGUAGE

About eight per cent of our communication is non-verbal. In our culture, a slight forward lean says, 'I'm listening'.

VERBAL FOLLOWING

This is the bit we haven't looked at before. It really means staying with the subject. Mostly we have a tendency in normal conversation to try to move things on. If we want to get deeper with young people we need to follow where they go in their conversations rather than introduce new topics that we feel safe with.

Below is an excerpt from a conversation with a young person:

Jane: My mum and me are going to the new shopping centre this weekend.

YW: Oh really—I went last week; they've got some great shops. I bought these boots from Miss Selfridge. Which shops do you like?

Jane: I like Snob, and Cult Clothing . . .

YW: Uh huh . . .

Jane: Yeah, and Miss Selfridge too. Any really. As long as Mum pays.

YW: Yeah?

Jane: Yeah.

As you can see, the conversation soon fades out. But why? The worker uses an open question and encouraging noncommittal responses, and yet still the conversation flags. The answer, of course, is that the worker has not really stayed with the subject.

Let's try it again:

Jane: My mum and me are going to the new shopping centre this weekend.

YW: Oh yeah, you and your mum?

Jane: Yeah, normally we don't get on but I thought I'd give it a go.

YW: Uh huh, what made you think you'd have a go?

Jane: Well we had lots of rows before Dad left but now he's gone it might be different.

YW: I didn't know your Dad had left. When did he go?

Jane: Oh, about two weeks ago.

YW: How do you feel about that . . .? (and so on . . .)

Now that was a conversation that could run and run. The way the youthworker stayed with the subject allowed Jane to talk about what was on her mind, and the conversation to deepen.

This staying with young people in what they want to talk about is what will distinguish an average youthworker from one who deeply cares about young people and who is prepared to listen to whatever they have to say for the sake of bringing them the gospel.

EXERCISE

Assess how good a listener you are by answering the following questions.

◆ **In an average conversation do you listen or talk more?**

◆ **How are you at staying with a topic?**

◆ **Do you have a tendency to swing conversation around to topics you know something about?**

◆ **Do you lean forward slightly when you are listening?**

◆ **Do you make good use of eye contact?**

Having answered these, ask a friend to answer the following.

◆ **Do you feel that I am better at listening or talking?**

◆ **Do I give the impression that I have plenty of time when you talk to me?**

◆ **Do I look at you when we talk?**

◆ **Would you say I stayed with topics of conversation or do I move conversation on to topics of interest to me?**

On the results of these two lots of answers, write yourself two hints to help you improve your listening skills.

EEDBACK

It is difficult to be objective, isn't it? Most people who are involved in working with people, or who do volunteer work with them, tend to think they are good listeners. Often this is not true. We may be able to listen well, or we may listen well if someone says, 'I want to talk.' But in everyday conversation we are likely to be poor at really giving our attention. It seems to me that this is because people like me, and I guess you too, are busy. We are busy saving the planet, or at least our corner of it. We are busy rushing from one person with a problem to another. So busy that we end up not using the very skills we are good at, that brought us into doing this kind of work in the first place! Having someone else assess you is not very comfortable, but often it is the best place to start. If we listen to what the person assessing us says we can learn a lot about ourselves, but it requires us to actively listen to them not just to hear what they say and still think that we know better.

You should now have two helpful suggestions to improve your listening skills. These should be short enough to keep in your head, so that when you are next with a young person you can say them over to yourself in your mind and they will help you to concentrate on what the person is saying. Listening to young people is so important. Imagine for a minute that no one had ever listened to you. How would you feel? Terrible. Being listened to is one of the things that gives us worth. To be worth listening to means you must be of some value and interest. Several of the young people I work with experience this kind of listening only very rarely. It is a vital part of our developing a relationship that I am different, that I will listen to them to the very best of my ability. This amount and depth of listening is difficult, tiring and time consuming, but it communicates care and love. I love young people as God helps me to, because God loves me. Listening is a way of showing it.

CONCLUSION

In this chapter I have attempted to share with you some insights into communicating with young people on an individual basis. It is this meeting of minds, this sharing of ideas with young people, that enables relationships to develop. If I am to talk about my faith I need to do it in the context of what I know about the young person, and I need to do it in terms that they understand, and are relevant. I cannot do this without these communication skills. As one of the young people I know said to me yesterday, 'Jude, you gotta be honest about what you think. We'll listen, 'cos we know you.' To get to know young people you've got to talk and you've got to listen. Happy communicating!

3 GROWING UP: THE INSIDE WORLD

Sam Adams

CONSTRUCTING A LIFE PLAN

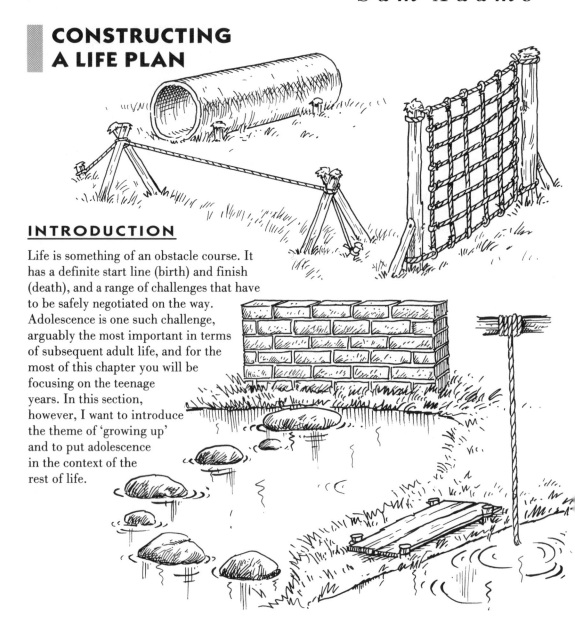

INTRODUCTION

Life is something of an obstacle course. It has a definite start line (birth) and finish (death), and a range of challenges that have to be safely negotiated on the way. Adolescence is one such challenge, arguably the most important in terms of subsequent adult life, and for the most of this chapter you will be focusing on the teenage years. In this section, however, I want to introduce the theme of 'growing up' and to put adolescence in the context of the rest of life.

XERCISE

In your notebook, I want you to construct a 'typical life-plan'. Give yourself a large area of paper (such as A4 size) and draw a line along the longest length in the middle of the page—this will be your time axis. Mark 'birth' at the left-hand end and 'death' at the right-hand end, as below:

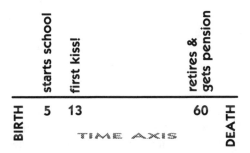

Now think of the young people that you work with, their families and their lives. Decide if you are going to work on a life-plan for a man or a woman, and call your 'typical' person Joe Bloggs or Joanne Bloggs accordingly! Then think of the major events in their life, and fill them in on your life-plan by marking the age (or approximate age) at which each event happens on the time axis, and writing the event above the line. For example:

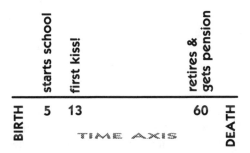

Spend fifteen minutes or so filling in your life-plan. Keep the area under the time axis clear—you will need to use this later! Remember you are making a quick

sketch—it is more important to cover the whole life span briefly than to complete one section in great detail.

XERCISE

Now look at your life-plan and think about the following questions—you can write comments in your workbook.

◆ Are there some ages or periods of life when more seems to be changing than at others?

◆ Was there an age beyond which it became more difficult to decide what would typically happen to someone?

◆ Would it have made any differences to your life-plan if you had chosen someone of the opposite sex?

Look at the various events and changes—can you sort these out into different types (you could mark them in different colours)? For example, things that happened to J. Bloggs over which they would have no choice, and things where they have a degree of choice (perhaps choice over when it happens, or if it happens). How else could you sort the various life events?

EEDBACK

I expect that your 'typical life-plan' looks pretty complicated by now! I find that I need more space for the early years when there are a lot of landmarks in growing up: starting to crawl, walk, talk, play with other children, go to toddler group and so on. For almost every year of life there seems to be new achievements in the process of growing up as a child. Once at school, this seems to slow down a little until teenage years when there are a whole new set of changes: starting to date, the physical changes of puberty, starting to earn money, school-work for public exams and so on.

Beyond the age of sixteen it often becomes more difficult to say what is typical. This is because up to that age the changes have been largely either the inevitable consequences of being a member of society (for example, experience of pre-school play group, age of starting school) or the results of normal physical and mental development. At age sixteen, however, there appears to be more choice and, therefore, more room for divergence. Whether to stay in education or not, what type of job to get, whether and when to leave home, whether and when to settle down with a partner, whether to have children— all of these choices affect the shape that one's life takes from that point onwards.

It is important to remember that not even these adult life-choices happen in a vacuum. Where we live, the state of the economy, our family's expectations, our natural talents and skills all have an effect upon what choices are actually available to us.

Towards the end of life, as old age sets in, the changes are again influenced by physical factors. As one's body loses strength and health, life often becomes more restricted due to reduced income and mobility.

EXERCISE

Now go back to your 'typical life-plan' and use the area under the time axis. Think about your own life up to this point, and fill in the major events and changes in your life. Take twenty minutes or so to do this.

Now spend some time looking at your life and the 'typical life-plan' you had compiled earlier based on the young people that you know. Comment in your workbook:

◆ **What are the main similarities?**

◆ **What are the main differences?**

FEEDBACK

The most obvious difference, I hope, is that your life doesn't extend as far as the right hand end of the axis—death! You may find that because the lower life-plan is based on a real life, it has more detail and includes events that are more personal or unique, for example, moving house, the birth of a younger sibling, someone dying and so on. When you were thinking about a 'typical life-plan', you may have assumed that life ran fairly smoothly, without any unnecessary traumas such as illness, relationships breaking up, or whatever. However most people experience their share of problems, and these will affect the whole process and experience of growing up.

It is important to be aware of the differences between our experiences of growing up and those of the young people with whom we work. For a start, we grew up in a different era! I grew up doing well at school and enjoying studying and, as expected, went on to higher education. I now work with young people from Blackbird Leys, Oxford, many of whom struggle with the academic side of school, and almost all of whom have no desire to go to university! I find I have to be careful not to assume that they are as I was at their age. It is very easy to fall into the mistake of trying to encourage them to have the same values and attitudes that I and my family had, rather than to discover what they themselves want from adult life and to encourage them towards their own goals and dreams.

EXERCISE

Now that you have spent some time thinking about growing up and your own experiences, it is worth asking *yourself* a few questions. Take ten minutes at the most, and write your answers in your workbook:

◆ **In other people's eyes I *look* as though I am _____ years of age.**

◆ **In my own eyes I judge my *body* to be like that of a person of about _____ years of age.**

◆ **My *thoughts and interests* are like those of a person about _____ years of age.**

◆ **My *position in society* is like that of a person about _____ years of age.**

◆ **Deep down inside, I really *feel* like a person about _____ years of age.**

◆ **And I would honestly *prefer* to be about _____ years of age.**

FEEDBACK

How did you find this exercise? Many people find it hard to pin themselves down to an age for each question—but it is a good discipline to do so.

How many different ages did you write down to describe yourself? How wide an age-span did they cover? Were any of the ages the same or very close to your actual age?

One of the aims of this exercise is to make you aware of how you feel about your own

stage in life, and the different factors that might affect this—how you look, your health and fitness, your thoughts and interests and your position in society. All of these things do change with age!

One of the great challenges of youthwork is that we, as youthworkers, have to bridge the generation gap in some way if we are going to be able to build meaningful relationships with young people. Just being aware of the differences between the stage of life you are in and the experiences and concerns of a teenager is a good start.

I look much younger than I am, and I generally dress casually. As a result, in the school where I do my youthwork, I am sometimes mistaken by the staff for a sixth-former. Now while this may be flattering (!) it is deceptive—because none of the young people would ever make that mistake. In their eyes I am clearly an adult. For all that I wear jeans and baggy tops, my style is not quite the same as theirs—and they are much more expert on what's in than I am!

More importantly, as soon as I sit down with a bunch of young people and listen to their conversation, it is clear to me that our interests are very different. The war in former Yugoslavia, the ordination of women and the price of wine in Sainsbury's rarely come up for discussion. We don't even seem to watch the same programmes on TV. And when they talk about music, it is not only that the bands we like are different, but the way we feel about them.

So it is up to me to take the time and effort required to bridge this gap if we are going to build any sort of relationship. There are various ways of doing this. I do find some young people with whom I naturally share an interest—for example mountain-biking, which I do one afternoon a week with some lads. I make some effort at least to recognize what is being talked about by watching occasional episodes of the soaps, reading teenage magazines I find lying around and listening to the radio. Above all, I try to extend my interest in a young person to their concerns and interests. This can mean suspending my own dislike for Take That, and enjoying a teenage girl's enthusiasm for the group. It often means listening much more than talking, and allowing the young people to be the experts on a subject they are explaining to me.

At the same time, it is important not to lose this generation gap—it is the very thing that makes us distinctive and unique as we become friends with young people. Our aim is to be an *adult* friend, and not just another teenage buddy. As adults we are able to offer young people:

◆ another perspective to that of their peers

◆ our own experiences—real life, first hand

◆ an example of adulthood—something to aim for

◆ proof that there is life after 20!

◆ a friendship robust enough to take the ups and downs of teenage moods

◆ and, of course, our faith.

XERCISE

Time for a little more reflection! Take ten minutes or so to answer the following three questions about why you do youthwork as honestly as possible:

◆ **What is your motivation?**

◆ **What is your reward?**

◆ **What does it cost you?**

Try to be as specific as you can— 'because God loves me' is not a sufficient answer to the first question!

EEDBACK

These are crucial questions to have answers to. The reason I have put them in a section looking at life's pattern is because often our own lives give us big clues.

For example, many people get involved in youthwork because:

◆ When they were a teenager, there was someone around who made a difference to their life, and they want to be able to offer that to young people now.

Or:

◆ When they were a teenager, they could have done with having someone around, but there wasn't anyone, so they now want to try to offer young people what they never had.

I have to say that I fall into the second of these categories. This might seem altruistic, and obviously that is a part of what is going on. But at another level, it is actually a way of meeting my own needs that were not met when I was younger. By offering care to others, I am also offering care to that part of myself, giving those old needs legitimacy.

In thinking about what we get out of the youthwork we do, it is important to evaluate how much we enjoy it! Obvious really, because if we're not enjoying spending time with young people, you can guarantee they won't be enjoying it much either. Many people enjoy the company of teenagers because:

◆ They feel they missed out on being a teenager for some reason, and so this is an opportunity to recapture a little of the fun of being young.

Or:

◆ They really enjoyed being a teenager, and this is a way of holding on to some of that, whilst actually getting older, by staying 'young at heart'.

I fall more into the first of these categories. I am much more self-confident now than I was as a teenager, so I am willing to have a go at things which scare me, but that I think I might enjoy (such as mountain-biking!), which I would never have done as a young person—and have a lot of fun as a result!

As you can see, motivation and reward are often closely linked. However, we do have to be careful that our needs are not dominating our relationships with young people. Although it is natural that we should receive as well as give in our youthwork, we need to make sure that the balance is always loaded towards giving, towards the young people and their needs. We are primarily engaged in youthwork because we want to offer care and support to young people. To keep this balance healthy, we need to be aware of our own needs, and to make sure that they are being met outside of our youthwork. If this is not the case, then we are in danger of emotionally exploiting the young people we know—and young people are too vulnerable for us to take this risk with their lives.

This brings us onto the cost of doing youthwork. The model for ministry of any kind that Christ gives us is one of sacrifice. St Paul talks of his life as being poured out like a drink offering. If our work is of Christ, we should expect it to cost us in some way and, as in the parable of the person building a tower (Luke 14:28–30), we need to decide before we start if we are willing and able to afford it.

My youthwork costs my time (and mostly fairly precious free-time), my energy, my limited spare cash (doing things with young people costs money!) and my privacy. These are the most obvious costs. Then there are the more subtle ones, for example the cost of rejection, of discovering that in practice I'm not as patient/forgiving/good-humoured as I think I am. And the cost of any Christian leadership/ministry—that of higher standards of behaviour being expected of me, because I now represent not just myself, but Christ and his church.

If this is something you'd like to think more about, here are some Bible references for passages about Christian leadership/ministry:

 1 Thessalonians 2

 1 Timothy 3

 2 Timothy 2:14–26

 2 Timothy 4:1–8

 Titus 1:5–9

 1 Peter 5

 Matthew 20:20–28

 1 Corinthians 9

 2 Corinthians 6:3–13

Now that we've looked at life in general, growing up in particular, and being a youthworker, it is time to move on and focus on the young people we are working with, their needs, their stage of life and their experiences. In the next section we begin by looking at what is happening to their bodies . . . and how this affects their feelings.

▌ BODY MATTERS

INTRODUCTION

Adolescence is the time when our bodies change dramatically. We grow from being physically children to being physically adult. Of course, this is a very natural and necessary process, but few people seem to enjoy it! This section will focus on what happens to our bodies during puberty, and why these changes are often so difficult to cope with.

XERCISE

In your workbook, draw an outline of a nude figure of someone of the opposite sex to yourself, and mark and label all the physical changes that normally happen in puberty. Take about fifteen minutes to do this. For example:

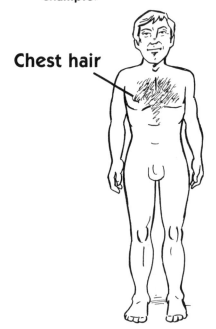

Chest hair

When you have finished, pick a good friend of that gender and ask them if you have left anything out!

EEDBACK

The first thing to say is that most people find this whole subject matter embarrassing—so if you wimped out of showing your drawing to anyone, don't worry! Sex and sexuality, for all that they are used to advertise everything under the sun, are tricky subjects to broach and most of us tend to avoid the whole thing. There are a number of reasons for this:

◆ It makes us feel very self-conscious.

◆ It raises all sorts of anxieties about how normal and attractive or otherwise we are.

◆ Because sexual attraction is such a powerful emotion, it feels scary and potentially dangerous.

◆ Sex is the source of our life, and it can be unnerving to realize our existence depended on so fragile and bizarre an act as our parents getting it together.

◆ For Christians there are added theological and moral factors which often result in less knowledge and experience in these areas.

If all of this is true for us as adult youth-workers, how much more so for the young people with whom we work. And this is the very reason why it is important that we can cope with our own feelings on the subject suffi-ciently to be able to be of help to a young person who is trying to sort out a personal problem.

So we must bite the bullet and get down to the facts and feelings of puberty.

NPUT

The physical changes of puberty are triggered by hormones, and the point of these changes is to turn a child into an adult capable of producing children themselves—that is with mature functioning genitals. Some of the effects of these hormones are temporary and affect both girls and boys—for example greasier hair, oilier skin that is more prone to spots, stronger smelling perspiration. Other effects are permanent, such as the growth of body hair, although in some different places on men and women!

The overall body shape changes. Before puberty, girls and boys have very similar bodies in terms of size, shape and strength (although obviously they have different genitals). In puberty, the bodies of the different genders start to take on their adult shape. Girls broaden at the hips and develop breasts. Boys broaden at the shoulders, develop 'Adam's apples' and lower voices, start to grow taller than girls and to develop bulkier muscles (this process continues for a number of years). In both sexes the genitals mature as well.

The biggest changes that both sexes have to deal with are connected to their new ability to reproduce.

GIRLS

In girls this means that their bodies begin to release ova (or eggs) from their ovaries and to prepare their bodies to carry a child, should this become fertilized, by thickening the womb lining. When each ovum is not fertilized, the body breaks down this material, and it is naturally passed out of the body with the ovum in the form of a blood-like excretion called menstruation (or a period). At first this is a very erratic occurrence, but the hormones that create these changes should settle down into a fairly regular pattern, often monthly, typically lasting between three and seven days.

For many girls, starting periods is a traumatic event. There are a number of reasons for this:

Physical. Periods often start out of the blue, so there is the problem of the unexpected excretion and how to deal with this, the embarrassment of stained clothing and so on. Periods are often accompanied by a degree of physical discomfort such as swollen breasts, back ache, stomach cramps and nausea. So having a period can be akin to being ill for a few days. The flow of menstrual blood may be quite heavy, making some normal activities difficult, such as swimming.

Degree of understanding. Depending at what age a girl starts her periods, and the attitudes of her school and parents, she may have very little knowledge or understanding about what is happening to her body. I know women who had been told nothing at all, who thought they were bleeding to death from some internal injury. I know women who knew a little about periods, but hadn't realized that the flow would be twenty-four hours a day! They thought that they would be able to stop it at will, or that it would stop at night.

Social taboos. In our culture it is not considered polite to talk about periods. Society expects women to cope with this everyday occurrence in such a way that nobody else need be aware of it: secretly, privately. It is interesting to note that although it is now acceptable to advertise tampons and sanitary towels on television and in magazines, advertisers do so in such a way as to promote their product without ever referring to its actual use! Or did you think that sanitary towels were made solely so women can pour glasses of blue tinted water onto them and talk about how absorbent they are?! The whole issue of menstruation is often treated as something dirty, disgusting and shameful (the feminist movement has fought to alter these attitudes), yet it is a normal and healthy part of life, and essential for the survival of our species. So most girls also have to deal with this social attitude, and how that makes them feel about themselves and their emerging womanhood, whilst often feeling unable to talk to other people about it all.

Practical. Every girl has to decide which form of sanitary protection she is going to use, and take responsibility for having enough and being prepared for unexpected periods. As girls can start menstruating as young as eleven (or occasionally even younger), this can be difficult to cope with.

Emotional. Because periods are the result of changes in hormone levels, many girls find that their emotions swing with the different phases of their menstrual cycle. This can be hard to cope with. Common experiences are feeling weepy or irritable for no apparent reason, giving rise to a sense of being unable to control one's emotional reaction to other people and events. Pre-menstrual tension or syndrome (PMT or PMS) is now a recognized medical phenomenon, and has been a proven factor in some cases of manslaughter—so these hormone-driven emotions can be very powerful and uncontrollable in some cases. For most young women, however, as their menstruation settles down to a more regular pattern or cycle, the emotional swings also settle down.

BOYS

For boys, the development towards genital maturity, and their ability to reproduce, focuses on the production of sperm and the natural way the body gets the sperm where it needs to be to successfully fertilize an egg or ovum. Once again, it is a change in the body's hormones which triggers the production of sperm in the testes (or balls). Once a young man has begun to produce sperm, this process continues into old age, and the sperm are kept ready for action in the testes. In order for these sperm to reach their goal, an ovum, the man's penis (or willy) must become firm (called an erection) so that he can enter a woman's vagina. It then acts as a tube which the sperm is pumped along, carried in a fluid called semen, into the woman's womb. This expulsion of semen is called ejaculation (or 'coming').

These two processes, erection and ejaculation, are vital for adult sexual intercourse and creating new life. The task of puberty, for most young men, is learning how to control these two new bodily functions. This can be a traumatic time for a number of reasons:

Physical. Erections are often uncontrollable! The penis is filled with blood, becomes much warmer, more sensitive and larger. It often feels tingly or throbby, and can stick out at strange and highly visible angles. It may get caught up in clothing, or suffer other damage, which can be very painful and embarrassing. Teenage boys may have as many as ten erections per hour in normal social settings (such as school), but this does decrease as they get older and more used to it all. Ejaculation also is a process over which teenage boys may have little control at first. Fortunately, this does not often happen without lots of warning signals! Ejaculation whilst sleeping (or 'wet dreams') can be quite common in puberty, but again tends to decrease with age and experience. Some young men use masturbation as a way of controlling the build up and release of sperm.

Degree of understanding. Depending on the age at which a boy starts to experience these things, and the attitudes of his school and parents, he may have very little knowledge or understanding about what is happening to his body. Men often describe it as suddenly finding that a part of your body appears to have a mind of its own. The 'Wicked Willy' cartoons contain a lot of truth! Boys often fear that they are becoming some sort of sex pervert as they struggle to control these new impulses.

Social taboos. There are a lot of myths around about male fertility, and the effects of masturbating (such as blindness!) which can be very confusing for a young man, whilst clear information is difficult to acquire. However, rather than not talk about these things at all, young men seem to deal with the issue by boasting of their male prowess and virility. It is inexperience that seems to be taboo.

Practical. Having an unwanted erection can be very embarrassing and painful, so young men have to learn ways of disguising it and of minimizing it (for example, thinking about completely non-sexual things like computer games or football). Wet dreams result in messy bedclothes, which often have to be explained to one's mum, or discreetly cleaned.

Emotional. Puberty can be an unnerving time for many young men. Emotional feelings and physical responses are very intertwined, and for the first time they are having to deal with sexual feelings and responses. They may find themselves turned-on without being consciously aware of why, or they may feel guilty about who they find attractive. These feelings can be very powerful and overwhelming, and boys may worry that they are becoming obsessed by their sexual feelings and reactions. Masturbation may also create confusing feelings of pleasure and release, and also guilt. It may be very difficult to find someone with whom these things can be discussed without fear of being ridiculed. For most young men, the intensity and erratic nature of these feelings settle down as they learn how to control their physical responses, and become more used to their new sexual awareness.

EXERCISE

We are starting to consider the prickly subject of gender, and what differences there are, if any, between men and women, male and female.

Re-read the section above on *Girls* and *Boys* and consider the following:

◆ **Do you agree with what I have said?**

◆ **Have I left anything important out? If so, what?**

◆ **How do your own experiences compare with these accounts?**

Now take about fifteen minutes and compile two lists, one headed *Male* and the other headed *Female*. Put in each list all the words that are commonly associated with that gender that you can think of. Don't worry about being 'right on' or politically correct at this point—the aim is to think about common assumptions, generalizations and archetypes.

For example:

Male	Female
macho	mother
DIY	caring
aggressive	makeup
etc.	etc.

Once you have made your two lists of words, see if you can group them together in any way, perhaps by marking them in different colours, or linking words together. Can you sort your words out into:

◆ **roles (e.g. mother, husband, etc.)**

◆ **character traits (e.g. aggressive, emotional, caring, etc.)**

◆ **associated activities (e.g. football, bingo, etc.)**

◆ **archetypes (e.g. Superman, Rambo, Marilyn Monroe, etc.)**

Now compare your two lists, *Male* and *Female*. Are there any similarities? What are the main differences?

 **EEDBACK**

This whole area is something of a minefield, as many people have very strong views about gender differences. By looking at common assumptions we are considering the views of our society on this issue, and not necessarily the actual differences between men and women. It is almost impossible to separate out the causes of the differences that we see into what is the result of nature and what is the result of nurture (the way we are brought up) and the views of the society within which we grow up.

We are left with the indisputable fact that there are two different genders, which Genesis 1 tells us were both created by God in his image, and that it takes both of these genders to create new life. So these two genders and their differences are complimentary.

Psychologists have found that it is very important for healthy adult life for individuals not to be ambivalent about their gender, but to have a firm sense of their sexuality and be at ease with it. We can think about this in terms of which team we belong to—the male team or the female team. This sense of belonging to one or other team begins in early childhood, but it is an issue that is still being worked out in the teenage years. Belonging to the team involves identifying yourself with other people of your gender (family, friends, TV characters and so on), and seeing yourself as different from the opposite team. This is made easier when there are obvious differences between the two teams (which may explain much of the social differences between men and women). As Robin Skynner says:

The child needs parents who share some activities and interests, and at least some of his care. But the child also needs them to be different, and stand for different things, and to respect and enjoy and admire each other's differences. You need TWO landmarks to get a bearing and find out where you are—and you need them to be a certain distance apart.

Robin Skynner and John Cleese,
Families and How to Survive Them,
Mandarin, 1983

As we grow up, we need to find out where we are, and build our gender identity. I would like to suggest that girls and boys have markedly different experiences of the physical changes of puberty, and that we may be able to find an explanation for some of the commonly observed psychological differences between men and women in this. It seems to me that in puberty girls have to come to terms with adapting their lives to cope with a bodily function over which they can have little control, that is menstruation. For boys, the task is rather one of gaining control over their body's new ability to create erections and to ejaculate. So for girls, becoming a woman has something to do with passive acceptance, whilst for boys becoming a man has to do with gaining mastery.

At the same time, it is not healthy when these differences become too rigid and over-exaggerated (something the church as well as society has been guilty of in the past). For example, when it is generally believed that real men never cry, or that women are incapable of making rational decisions, we limit people's basic expression of their humanity by forcing them into restrictive roles if they want to be accepted members of their team. And when society values its definition of one gender above the other, we have created a system of repression and abuse that is as pervasive and powerful as apartheid.

As adults entering the lives of young people, we inevitably play a role in this process of sorting out gender identity. We can help by affirming them in their femininity and masculinity—but we can only do this if we ourselves are positive and comfortable with our own gender identity and enjoy the differences between ourselves and the other team. Good adult models of the same sex and of the opposite sex are vital, and sadly many young people do not have these available to them within their family home.

In adolescence, sorting this issue out is complicated by the arrival of sexual thoughts and feelings, triggered by the sex hormones released in puberty. And both sexes begin to be turned on by the increasingly adult shape of the other team, and form romantic attachments.

XERCISE

Birds do it, bees do it, even educated fleas do it . . . Falling in love is a natural and wonderful part of life. And teenagers do it left, right and centre. They fall in love with pop stars, sporting heroes, TV actors, each other and, from time to time, youthworkers.

Handling a teenage crush is a tricky business. For starters, it may be very flattering and we need to be able to

cope with our own anxieties about the situation as well as the teenager's strong feelings without jeopardizing the relationship.

Here is a scene from *Pale Rider* (Warner Brothers)—a movie set at the turn of the last century in a frontier mining village. Imagine a typical Western, with Clint playing a mysterious 'preacher' staying with a family, and the teenage daughter falls in love . . .

Girl: I buried my dog over here [shows Clint].

Clint: That's hallowed ground then.

Girl: I said a prayer for her—it was after the raid. I prayed for a miracle.

Clint: Well maybe someday you'll get that miracle.

Girl: It was the day you arrived . . . I think I love you.

Clint: There's nothing wrong with that. If there was more love in the world there'd probably be a lot less dying.

Girl: Then there can't be anything wrong with making love either.

Clint: I think it's best to just practice loving for a while before you think about the other.

Girl: If I practice just loving for a while, will you teach me the other?

Clint: Megan, most folks around kinda associate that with marriage.

Girl: I'll be fifteen next month— momma was married when she was fifteen. Will you teach me then?

Clint: Ninety-nine out of a hundred men would be proud to say yes to that, Megan. But a young girl— young woman like you, you wouldn't want to spend your future with a man like me.

Girl: Why not?

Clint: That's just the way it is.

Girl: I don't understand . . . I don't believe you . . . I don't want to believe you . . . [throws arms around Clint, sobbing]. Whatever you say isn't true . . . isn't fair.

Clint: Come on now—that's no way to pass the test.

Girl: [draws away] Test?

Clint: Trust—if you love someone, you've got to try to trust that what they tell you is true.

Girl: Even if it means they can't be together?

Clint: One day a young man is going to come along, the right man, and none of this will matter anymore. Now, if I was your mom, I'd be worried about where you are.

Girl: It's my momma you love, isn't it?

Clint: Your momma's a fine woman, and so are you.

Girl: The way you look at her and the way she looks at you [getting angry]. It's true . . . I don't care—you can have her! I never want to see you again!

Clint: Megan . . .

Girl: I hope you die and I hope you go to hell [stomps off].

Well—how would you rate him as a youthworker? In your notebook, write a critique of how he handles this delicate situation. You might find it helpful to consider the following questions:

◆ **What should be his aims in this encounter?**

◆ **How does he respond to the girl at different stages?**

◆ **How does he try to contain the emotional outpourings?**

◆ **How does the language he uses affect the impact of what he says?**

◆ **What messages do you think he is trying to give the girl?**

◆ **Why does she stomp off at the end?**

◆ **Was he successful?—refer to your original aims.**

◆ **How would you have handled things differently?**

◆ **Can you draw any lessons from this for your own youthwork?**

Take half an hour to work through this scene, reading it through a few times and getting your ideas on paper, before reading the feedback!

FEEDBACK

Overall, I think he does pretty well.

A key aim in this sort of situation is to avoid damaging the self-esteem of the young person if at all possible, whilst giving them the clear message that you are not going to enter into any kind of intimate and sexual relationship with them. *Always remember that you are the adult*—and therefore your self-esteem should be much less fragile than that of the young person and need less protecting. The young person has taken a big risk in letting you know that they have a crush on you, either by words or actions, and it is vital that you do respond. To say or do nothing and hope it just goes away is to duck the issue for our sakes, to avoid putting ourselves on the line. This can be very confusing for a young person, who may read all sorts of things into your silence. Remember what it is like to 'fall in love'—every glance, gesture and word is invested with enormous meaning if there is no evidence to the contrary. So it is very important to be giving a clear 'no' message, whilst at the same time continuing to offer the supportive friendship as always.

Clint never goes onto the defensive—he never puts Megan down in order to protect himself. He doesn't even deny that it is her mother he is after—because that is actually irrelevant. We shouldn't justify our feelings for one person by talking about our feelings for someone else. That only gives the impression that should circumstances change, your feelings might change. For example, if I explain to a young man that the reason I won't go out with him is because I already have a boyfriend, I may leave him with the impression that should this relationship end, I might change my mind. In fact, what I want to communicate to the young man is that I will only ever offer him friendship.

It is important not to be patronizing in our response. Clint is trying not to treat her as a child, although he has to correct his language, when referring to her, from 'young girl' to 'young woman'. It is very important that the young person does not feel ridiculed, but rather taken seriously. It is when he again refers to her as a child—'if I was your mom, I'd be worried about where you are'—that she stops listening to what he is saying, and starts to find her own reasons for his reaction to her.

Where possible, without getting ourselves into deep water, we should still aim to build up the young person's self-esteem and to affirm their sexuality and attractiveness. I think Clint does pretty well on these scores. Nowadays, this can be complicated by the worry of abuse allegations, but it is important not to allow our professional worries to prevent us from responding positively for the young person's sake.

It is important to give young people the message that you think love is good (after all God is love) and that the ability to love is one of the most precious things we can have as humans. I think Clint manages to do this!

We don't want our negative response to put them off the whole idea. In fact, an incident like this could give you an opportunity to explore the whole theme of *love* with the young person or group of them. C.S. Lewis's ideas on the four different types of love might be a good starting point.

Teenagers feel things very strongly. In the film scene, the girl moves from undying love to tears to anger within a very few minutes. And this is normal!! In fact, stomping off at the end was a way for her to regain some power in the situation, having earlier made herself very vulnerable. We should expect this sort of defensive behaviour, and try not to take it personally.

Overall, I think Clint handles the situation pretty well. We need to remember that there is no perfect, sure-fire way of dealing with this sort of thing. If you manage as well as he does, you're doing more than OK.

SUMMARY

Body matters in adolescence are all about teenagers' emerging sexuality. Coming to terms with the physical changes can be difficult, but most people arrive out the other side of this period as normal and healthy adults. The physical changes heighten issues around masculinity and femininity. Along with all of this, feelings of sexual love are often being experienced for the first time. In this world of confusing new sensations and ideas, we try to offer young people accepting friendship, the opportunity to have access to information and support as they form their sexual identities.

This is an important part of the whole process of identity formation that dominates the teenage years, which we will explore in the next section. But have a well-earned break before that!

SO WHO AM I ANYWAY?

INTRODUCTION

Who am I? This is one of life's biggest questions, and it is in adolescence that we both start to pose the question and try to find an answer.

So that you have some real-life material to relate to the ideas we are going to explore in this section about our identity and how we form it, I would like you to undertake a simple self-survey.

XERCISE

On a sheet of paper, write down fifteen different answers to the question 'Who am I?' Each answer should begin 'I am . . .' Try to describe yourself as fully as you can in your fifteen answers. Don't worry about what anyone else would think of your answers—this exercise is about how you see yourself. Just put down whatever comes to mind, and don't worry if your answers seem inconsistent or unimportant. Try to take no more than ten minutes to do this.

For example:

1   I am only 5'2"

2   I am a Christian

3   I am a trainer of youthworkers

4   I am a good team member

5   I am creative

and so on

EEDBACK

Have a look at your answers—and if you haven't done the exercise, go back and do it now! You may well find that you can sort your answers into three broad categories:

NOUNS

These describe various roles, positions and groups which you associate with yourself. Some may describe your relationship to different people and various roles that you take—for example, father, wife, best friend, boss, volunteer. Others describe your particular skills and hobbies—for example, golfer, knitter, artist, pilot. Yet others may describe formal or informal groups to which you belong—for example, Liverpool fan, Baptist, train spotter, feminist, Conservative. Nouns describe who we are mostly by what we do and the roles we play. These help us both to feel we are members of the human race, because of our membership of these various sub-groups, and to feel that we are uniquely ourselves because the combination of these nouns is our own particular blend of roles, group loyalties and abilities, and there are very few other people for whom they would all be true.

ADJECTIVES

These describe personal attributes and personality traits you see within yourself—for example, creative, competitive, lazy, underpaid, optimistic, insecure, happy-go-lucky, tall, overweight and so on. These may need some explanation, for example which areas of your life these apply to. These adjectives may give a clearer picture of how you *feel* about yourself than the nouns. How many of them do you think are positive qualities, and how many negative? This emotional or affective part of self-concept is usually called self-esteem.

COMBINATIONS OF ADJECTIVES AND NOUNS

For example, safe driver, happily married, reluctant choir-member, energetic youth-leader, bored housewife, gorgeous red-head, mad party-goer. These provide both facts and feelings about your identity.

There may, of course, be some answers that don't fit neatly into any of these categories—don't worry, that's just your uniqueness showing through!

 NPUT

IDENTITY

Identity is the mind's-eye picture we have of ourselves. It is one of the things that distinguishes us from animals and young children, who seem to have very little conscious awareness of their existence at all! It is important to have as sharp and well-focused an image of ourselves as possible. We may not like all we see, but at least we know what's there. This helps us:

◆ to know that we are special and unique— vital for good self-esteem and a foundation of the Christian faith. We all need to feel that we matter and are worth something.

◆ to know what to expect from ourselves—a huge asset in an uncertain world, one less thing to worry about. We are then free to concentrate on other people's actions and external circumstances. We are able to rely on who we are, and our responses, and have a sense of being a coherent and consistent person. A clear sense of identity enables us to make decisions and act boldly.

Adolescence is the period of our lives when we build the basic framework of our identity, and start to test its strength. This identity needs to be robust enough and yet flexible enough to see us through the rest of our life with its many stresses and crises. It also needs to be solid enough for us to risk venturing into intimate relationships, when we allow others to get to know who we really are, or to express our identity in creative effort and show who we are to the outside world.

It is in our teens that we begin to have an inner sense of who we are for the first time. It is very common for teenagers to start to examine the roles that they play and the different ways they behave in different settings and especially around different groups of people, and to feel that they have split personalities. They feel they are one person at school with their friends, and quite another at home with their family. Young people often report feeling something of a chameleon, that who they are seems to be fluid and adapt to the setting and people around. Whilst this can be upsetting and unsettling, it is quite normal, and usually fades with time as the young person becomes surer of their answer to the crucial question of adolescence: Who am I?

This growing sense of unity, of being a whole, rounded person, is a vital ingredient in another development at this time—fidelity. This is a new-found ability in adolescence to be able to be faithful to a person, an idea, an opinion or a cause. This is an important aspect of our identity—what we think, what we like and dislike, what we value and what we believe. It is in adolescence that we make commitments to these as core parts of who we are.

This is one of the reasons why youthwork is so exciting. The young people we are getting to know are in the very process of forming the basis of their adult identity, and so are looking for ideas, opinions, theories and people worth believing in, worth basing their very selves upon and being faithful to.

WARNING!

Just in case you are about to get carried away on a wave of evangelistic fervour, a few points to bear in mind:

◆ It is for these very reasons that young people are particularly at risk from cults and other such groups who 'sell' an answer to life. As Christian youthworkers we need to make sure that our methods are honouring to the young person and to God, and that we do not take advantage of minds much more mouldable than our own, of personalities much more fragile and lives much more needy, in our desire to guide young people into faith.

◆ Teenagers are still in the process of growing up, and faith may be one of the things they reject and leave behind in the world of childhood on their way into adulthood. We need to be offering a faith that grows and matures with them, rather than one that is easily outgrown as the rest of life changes around them. This means being prepared to be around and support teenagers who may be radically challenging our beliefs as they test that faith out for themselves and its ability to meet the new demands of their ever-changing lives.

◆ We are still working with teenagers—even if everything goes swimmingly, and they get into God as a result of having us around. Fidelity is a new ability, and we need to expect teenagers to be beginners at it! Picture a baby that is just learning to walk—every step is a major achievement, and every falling down a necessary part of the learning. So we should expect teenagers to do their fair share of falling down in this area as in every other. Teenagers are unreliable, and it is foolish to expect them to be anything else—whilst always encouraging them to become reliable and, more importantly, faithful! Is now the time to mention that you have to be a saint to be a youthworker?!

Having said all of the above, it is still true that adolescence is a crucial time in a person's life, when they start to question and look for answers to life that will become a part of who they are. If we are significant people in the lives of young people, then we can expect to play a part in this searching process, and be able to offer our own ideas and beliefs. The young person is then free to consider these in the light of what they know about us as people and in the light of their own values and beliefs. And many young people come to faith for the first time as teenagers as a result of this very interaction.

EXERCISE

Having got this far, let's construct a model for *identity*, so we have an idea of the scale and breadth of the task that adolescents are undertaking in forming and consolidating their identity.

Begin by spending ten minutes or so brainstorming the different things that go make someone who they are, the various elements of our identity. A good place to start is to look back at your personal answers to the last exercise, and to generalize from that. For example, if you put 'I am a father', you could write 'family relationships' and 'personal responsibilities' in your list of general components of identity. Another example: if you put 'I am ambitious', you could write 'future expectations' and 'personal temperament' on your brainstorm list. Once you've exhausted your answers, see if there are any other things you can add to your list.

Now look at your general list, and group the words together into related areas of identity. You should end up with quite a few sub-sets of words, for example things related to appearance (looks, style, height, colour), background (race, culture, family and so on), social status (age, job, income and so on), ethics (beliefs, values, opinions, attitudes) and personal traits (skills, interests, hobbies, temperament). You may well find that some of the words belong to more than one area, for example race is related to appearance, background and status—clearly our identity is complex, and our model will reflect that by areas overlapping. What about gender—where does that fit into your model?

Adolescence is the time in our lives when we get our teeth into the question of 'Who am I?' This exercise shows the many areas involved in starting to answer that question, and to some degree it is a question we continue to address for the rest of our lives. However, it is vital that we emerge from our teenage years with a good enough answer to this question to be able to get on with the rest of our lives. The answer we find at this stage is our working basis for adulthood, and it is this answer that we amend and adjust as the result of our experiences as we grow older.

INPUT

SELF-CONCEPT

How we feel about who we are is a crucial factor in all of this. Our self-esteem is basically a measure of how much we like ourselves. Common sense and everyday dealings with people tell us that low self-esteem is not good for people, and greatly reduces their ability to enjoy life and relate well to other people; whilst high self-esteem gives people self-confidence and self-assurance, enabling them to take risks, receive criticism, be more open with people and be less easily swayed by outside pressure.

There are four key elements to our self-esteem:

A sense of moral worth. Everyone needs to feel confident that they are basically an OK person. We all need to know that we will act in a good or upright way when confronted with an ethical choice. Now different people obviously have very different definitions of 'good', and different ethical frameworks within which they judge themselves and others. But the need to believe we are one of the good guys is universal, and fundamental to our self-esteem.

Guilt undermines this. Now we are getting into theologically murky waters. As Christians, we can be sure of our OK-ness through Christ's redemption and forgiveness, yet we still experience a struggle in the area of our own goodness.

For I have the desire to do what is good, but I cannot carry it out. For what I do is not the good I want to do; no, the evil I do not want to do—this I keep on doing.

St Paul in Romans 7:18–19 (NIV)

This is even more complicated when thinking about non-Christians. How do we as youthworkers tackle the issue of someone's low self-esteem if they do not have the assurance of God's approval? I'll leave you to chew that one over for the time being.

A sense of competence. We all need to know that there are some things in life we're pretty good at, some areas in which we feel successful. Our sense of competence is determined by the ratio between our level of ability and our level of expectation. That is, our self-esteem will increase if our skill, or our degree of success rises on the one hand, or our hopes or pretensions are scaled down on the other. For example, if I hope to swim fifty lengths but only manage thirty, my self-esteem sinks; however if I hope to swim twenty-five and achieve thirty, I feel positively buoyant! What often happens is that as our skill increases, our expectations of ourselves rise even faster, so we remain discouraged, being our own worst critics.

A sense of self-determination. We all need to feel that we have some power to control and change our lives. People who feel their lives are ruled entirely by fate, or by others around them, have a low image of themselves, and consequently no energy with which to stand up for themselves. People who feel able to accept responsibility for their lives, to make decisions, to give opinions and to take action will feel much more positive about themselves as people.

A sense of unity. We all need to feel that we are basically a consistent person—that our feelings, beliefs and actions add up to one whole person, rather than parts of a variety of people.

If all of these elements are in place, we will be comfortable with who we are, and will probably basically like ourselves. If they are not, our internal support is lacking, and we are more likely to suffer from a lack of self-esteem.

EXERCISE

Most adolescents suffer from low self-esteem, either for a short period of time as they grow up, or for the whole of their teenage years. Look back at the four key elements of good self-esteem, and list particular reasons why this is so at their stage of life. Take fifteen or so minutes to do this.

Understanding the problem should help us to become part of the solution. Given what you have deduced about the problems of self-esteem for teenagers, how could you start to address those issues through your relationship with them as a Christian youthworker? What resources do you have to offer? What does the gospel bring to this area of life? Take another fifteen minutes or so to come up with some answers specific to your own youthwork. It might help to think of individual young people you know, those who are obviously lacking in self-assurance, and those who seem to be OK.

FEEDBACK

This is a vital issue to tackle in our ministry to young people. Low self-esteem can be the root of all kinds of problems in someone's life, from promiscuity to under-achieving in exams, and above all robs people of their enjoyment of life in all its fulness. It is a disease that strikes indiscriminately, across all sections of society, and affects both Christians and non-Christians alike.

Let's look at some of the specific factors that undermine self-esteem in adolescence:

A sense of moral worth. Teenagers are still in the process of defining what is 'good' for themselves, and while this remains vague it is much harder to feel they are OK without a reliable measure to use. Teenagers are often experiencing sexual feelings for the first time, and may feel uncomfortable about this and therefore not OK. Teenagers are often busy rejecting the rules and values of authority as they try to find their own, and so can be on the receiving end of someone else's definition of them as immoral (for example, school, police, parents).

A sense of competence. It is as teenagers that our competence is formally assessed by examiners, against a standard that is impersonal. There is often very little outside recognition for the things that teenagers strive to be competent at, such as the latest style of dance. Feeling incompetent is a negative spiral for the self-conscious teenager—lack of achievement leads to unwillingness to risk having a go for fear of embarrassment.

A sense of self-determination. Teenagers often feel that they are being asked to make decisions that they feel incapable of and ill-equipped for (such as school options, career choice, which parent to live with following a break up), whilst not being given the freedom to make the choices they want to about their lives (such as how late to stay out, how to approach simple tasks and so on). They often feel trapped within other people's expectations of them.

A sense of unity. Teenagers often find their own reactions unpredictable, partly the result of hormones, and partly just the result of being half-way between childhood and adulthood. Others often find them unpredictable and changeable too! This, plus the chameleon-feeling mentioned earlier, can threaten their sense of unity.

How other people respond to us. This is an over-riding factor in self-esteem for all of us. Positive response improves our self-concept, negative response reduces our self-concept. We form our self-images by seeing ourselves through the eyes of others, and how they define, label and attribute meaning to our lives. For example, they may see us as:

◆ flexible or wishy-washy

◆ firm or stubborn

◆ courageous or foolhardy

◆ sensible or chicken

◆ generous or wasteful

◆ thrifty or tight-fisted

◆ enthusiastic or unstable

◆ steady or dull.

from Em Griffin, *Making Friends and Making Them Count*

This, then, is a big clue as to what we can do as positive adults in the lives of young people. St Paul tells us to 'build one another up in love', and we should aim to build up young people, to increase their self-esteem.

A sense of moral worth. We can begin by showing the young person that they are of worth, that we value them regardless of their actions (that good old approach of 'love the sinner not the sin'). After all, the gospel starts with the fact that God so loved us that he sent his only son to die for our sins. We don't become of worth to God after we become Christians—it is because we are so precious to him that he gives us the opportunity in the first place.

A sense of competence. We can try to offer teenagers opportunities to develop their competence, by giving them tasks within their capabilities, safe places to try new things with no fear of ridicule, and appropriate praise for their successes.

A sense of self-determination. We can try to offer teenagers opportunities to express their opinions, to make choices and bring about changes. We need to be aware of how much power we hold in our relationship with them, and offer to share that equally with them.

A sense of unity. We can offer reliable feedback to them about who they are, and how they come across to others in different situations, and thereby help them to bring their sense of who they are into sharper focus. Building others up needs to be a conscious effort on our part, and every little positive remark really does count.

These are just a few general ideas. I hope that you are able to turn these into specific things that you can do as a youthworker. Pick three of your ideas which relate to particular young people you know, and give yourself the challenge of trying them out over the next week or two. Then come back to your work from this section, and assess how helpful it has been. Has it improved your ability to serve young people?

GROWING UP—MOVING ON

INTRODUCTION

This is the final section looking at the inner world of adolescence. We shall be pulling together some of the ideas we've explored so far, and thinking about the natural result of this period of growing up—moving on.

NPUT

Let's start by thinking back to the life-plan you constructed in the first section of this chapter. One way to think about life's pattern is in terms of dependency and independence. Below I have drawn a rough graph of dependency over a typical life:

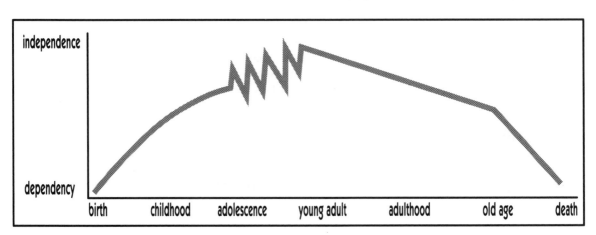

At birth we are completely dependent on the people who take care of us (usually our parents) for everything we need to live—food, warmth, shelter, love, safety and so on. As we grow up as children, we learn how to take care of ourselves in lots of different ways, whilst still being dependent on the adults around us for many things, especially love and support.

In adolescence, we seem to set our sights on adulthood, often seen in terms of complete independence, especially from parents and others in authority. It can be a very rocky road towards this goal, full of steps forward in terms of taking responsibility for a new area in one's life, and steps back to the security of being a child and having others take responsibility for you. It can seem a bit like 'bungy-running': spurts of frantic movement towards more independence with the pull of the elastic dragging us backwards every now and then. This process can turn into something of a pitched battle against parents and other authority figures. In the end, most of us achieve enough independence to become adults.

Adulthood usually involves building long-term relationships with other adults, and this includes depending on each other—a new phase of interdependency. Through having children, promotions at work or involvement in social activities, most people find that they have other people dependent on them to some degree and as one's parents age they may also become increasingly dependent.

Old age and increasing infirmity mean growing dependency on other people to take care for us.

How does this pattern fit with your 'typical life-plan' from the first section?

XERCISE

I have highlighted dependency and independence as things which mark a difference between childhood and adulthood. Take fifteen minutes to brainstorm two lists in your workbook—one for childhood and one for adulthood—of words that you associate with the two stages of life, thinking especially about the differences. For example:

Childhood	Adulthood
play	work
innocent	cynical

FEEDBACK

Adolescence is the transition from childhood to adulthood. The young people you work with are in the process of negotiating this change. How they view both childhood and adulthood will affect this process. Some young people clearly don't want to grow up (the Peter Pans of this world) whilst others are desperate to be seen as adults and ape adult styles, behaviour and so on, although often unsuccessfully and even comically.

Look again at your list of words:

◆ How many positive and negative words are there in each list? Mark them with a plus or minus sign. You may decide some words are neutral, which you can leave blank. What do the number of plus signs and minus signs tell you about your own views of childhood and adulthood?

◆ How many of the words are connected to the way society defines adulthood, for example by legal minimum ages to smoke, drive, have sex and so on?

◆ Can you think of any words the young people you know would add to these lists? It might be interesting to ask them to do this same exercise.

Adulthood is the goal we set for young people. We can think of growing up as leaving the 'country' of childhood and journeying to the land of adulthood. There are different customs in both places, and the route between them might be long and difficult. But how does a young person know when they have arrived at adulthood? In Western culture there are surprisingly few border checkpoints. Many other cultures have rites of passage or initiation processes which mark the arrival of adulthood. Does your list for adulthood contain any such 'checkpoints'?

Independence is a good measuring-stick for the achievement of adulthood. There are many areas of life involved in independence. Some are listed below:

◆ financial

◆ emotional

◆ social

◆ intellectual

◆ legal

◆ mobility.

EXERCISE

Choose two young people that you know fairly well, and write 'pen-portraits' of the degree to which they are independent. For example:

'SARAH'

Sarah is fifteen. She lives with her mum and stepdad, and their three younger children, on a council estate. She is dependent on them for her home (shelter, food, warmth, etc.) and the threat of being thrown out during an argument is a real worry. She has a weekend job, and seems to have complete freedom as to what she spends her money on. Legally she has to go to school, although she does skive, and her mum tends to back her up if teachers question her absence from school. In her spare time she often has to look after the other (younger) children at very short notice, but otherwise can do more or less as she pleases. She chooses her own friends and boyfriends, but does listen to her

mum's opinions about them. She is exploring the Christian faith on her own (that is, not as part of a group of friends) and frequently demonstrates her independence of mind (views, opinions and so on). Her father lives abroad, and she travels by herself to visit him. She is close to her mum, and missed her when she was recently in hospital.

Spend ten minutes or so writing each of your 'pen-portraits'. How do your young people compare with Sarah? In which areas are they more independent, and in which areas less so? What do you think are the reasons for this?

FEEDBACK

Independence is a complex issue! You may have found areas of life which it affects that aren't in my list above. The factors affecting how independent someone is may include:

◆ age

◆ the law (e.g. independence of mobility after passing a driving test is only possible after reaching age seventeen)

◆ the economic climate (e.g. the availability of jobs and housing for financial independence)

◆ educational choices (e.g. the decision to stay on at school past age sixteen)

◆ cultural traditions (e.g. many Asian girls have no freedom in their use of social/ spare time)

◆ gender

◆ personal maturity (think back to the last section on 'identity')

◆ family situation (e.g. responsibilities/ roles within the family).

INPUT

It is the last of these factors, the family, which we will now focus on. If one of the major tasks of adolescence is to achieve independence, then this is primarily experienced as independence from the family within which they have grown up. Independence here is about being our own person, whilst perhaps remaining an adult member of that family—it doesn't necessarily mean physically leaving the family. We are now talking about psychological independence.

Indeed, it has been proposed that asserting our right to a separate existence can unconsciously feel as if we are killing our parents and that therefore most— maybe all—of us (and especially those of us with clingy parents) have some degree of separation guilt. It has also been proposed that separation guilt is appropriate, that growing up is a form of homicide and that the assumption of responsibility for one's own life and its conduct is in psychic reality tantamount to the murder of the parents. Thus, by becoming autonomous (instead of remaining dependent), by establishing inner restraints (instead of needing our parents to serve as our external conscience), by cutting emotional ties (instead of seeking our gratifications within the family), by taking care of our needs (instead of surrendering that care to our mother and father), we annihilate our parents' roles and take them into ourself.

And, in that sense, are guilty of killing our parents.

**Judith Voist, *Necessary Losses,*
Simon & Schuster, 1988, page 148**

This process of 'killing our parents' or at least killing our need for parents, is the root of all the commonly experienced difficulties between parents and teenagers. There is something of an inevitable battle going on here. There is lots of scope for clashes between both sides as this conflict works its way out. Parents aren't necessarily willing to give their teenage children the freedom they want; teenagers aren't necessarily ready for the freedom they may be given. It is an immensely difficult time for both parties. Parents experience their teenagers as very changeable: one minute angrily disagreeing with everything they say, the next minute wanting reassurance and perhaps a cuddle!

We must remember that a part of the teenage experience is close to bereavement—the death of their childhood and the end of their family life which has been the mainstay of their existence up until then. Teenagers seem to try to make the task of leaving the safety of the parental home easier for themselves by persuading themselves that what they are separating from isn't that great anyway (to lessen the sense of loss) by finding fault with their parents. There is also a battle inside the teenager, who is trying to build some psychological distance from the family (which is a scary thing to do), whilst often needing the emotional support of the family to do this! It is all most confusing, and often errupts in arguments and a general feeling of not being understood at all. But this is all normal, and most of us survive to tell the tale, or more likely to try and forget about what is was like as quickly as possible.

Growing up in general, and adolescence in particular, is about increasingly being able to take care of ourselves rather than be reliant on our parents or other carers. This makes sense—as we become adult we need to become able to look after our own needs (or at least be aware of them and be able to ask for help we may need), so that we will one day be able to extend care to others (for example our own children!).

EXERCISE

Look again at your 'pen-portraits' and ask the question—to what extent have these young people annihilated their parent's roles and taken them into themselves?

For example, 'Sarah':

◆ **How autonomous is she?**

She seems to be about half-way there—she makes the most of all the opportunities to be autonomous that she is offered (for example going away to visit her father, getting involved with God), but she is still dependent on her family for some things.

◆ **To what degree has she established inner restraints?**

This is tricky to assess, because it is not clear that her family ever offered much in the way of external conscience. There are many issues in her life where she had no rules or guidelines, but she is in the process of creating her own, for example regarding sexual relationships. In other areas, there are family expectations, for example being available to look after the younger children, and she is often in conflict with her parents over this. The battle is about who has the right to define the rules now that she is growing up.

◆ **To what degree has she cut emotional ties?**

I'd take a rough stab at two-thirds! Sarah's friends and boyfriends play a more important role in her emotional life now than her family does. She also looks outside the family for adults (such as myself!) to talk to about problems and joys in her life. I would say that she is perhaps rather ahead of some of her peers in this—probably because she was closer to her father than her mum, and now lives with her mum and rarely sees her father. Her growing faith is another channel for her emotional life outside of the family. Having said all this, she does still talk to her mum about many things and finds her mostly supportive.

◆ **To what degree does she take care of her own needs?**

More than you might think, given that she still lives at home. She is aware of her needs, and does ask for help and advice when she needs it. Also, having to care for her young siblings has given her experience of taking care herself.

Now re-read the quotation from Judith Voist, and answer the same questions for your two young people. How do they compare with Sarah? Take twenty minutes or so to do this.

INPUT

By now you should be building up a clear picture of the extent to which two young people that you know are achieving independence and moving on from a life based around their family. Already, I am sure, you are discovering some of the *ways* in which young people negotiate this transition from dependence to independence.

Most young people use various forms of stepping-stones to bridge the gap between leaving the family as their main source of care and support on one side, and arriving at an adult ability to meet their own needs for care and support on the other side. In an ideal world, home and family life should act as a firm launch pad for blast off into adult life. Even when this is so, most young people need somewhere else to go, in the short term, to receive some of the good things they used to get from their families, and so they are now looking outside those families for new sources of support and care. We are now going to take a brief look at some of the most common stepping-stones that are used along the way. (We will look more closely at some of these things in chapter 7.)

PEER FRIENDSHIP GROUPS

YOUTH CULTURE

GIRLFRIENDS/ BOYFRIENDS

HIGHER EDUCATION

HOBBIES AND CAUSES

CAREER

PEER FRIENDSHIP GROUPS

One of the first places outside of the family that young people turn to as they grow up and move on is their friendships. It is in early adolescence that these friendships start to compete for importance with the family in the life of a young person. The need to be accepted, to be liked and to belong are transferred from home to these friendships. Young people tend to have a variety of levels of friendship, from large, loose groups they belong to, to small tight-knit groups of a few friends, to best-friends. These relationships may be short-term or very long-lived. Particularly in close friendships, many personal feelings may be expressed as they experience growing up together. Teenagers increasingly meet their social needs away from family life and in the company of their peers.

YOUTH CULTURE

One of the functions of 'youth culture' is to create some distance between teenagers and their parents. When Bob Geldof was a teenager, his father described the Rolling Stones as 'a bloody racket!' Bob Geldof writes:

That racket was the first thing I'd ever heard that felt like someone knew what IT felt like. They were indecipherable to parents, there was no mutual point of contact, but my father made the mistake of trying to appreciate the music. Appreciate! The whole point was that he couldn't ever. Parents should never try to understand. I wanted something of my own. Something SO totally MINE, and incomprehensible to the older people, they could never take it from me, because they didn't know what it was. They only knew that it irritated them, but they weren't sure why. It wasn't just the music, it was because they couldn't get to me. When I listened to it, I was lost to them. Like Elvis said, 'Let's get real gone fellas'. I went.

Bob Geldof, *Is That It?*, Penguin, 1986

So the music, fashions, language of teenagers all help in the process of separating from their parents. It can provide a sense of being OK, of being understood at a time when a teenager's family might well not understand, or when accepting that sort of understanding from one's parents might undermine the process of leaving them. Youth culture helps young people to create a world that is totally their own.

GIRLFRIENDS/ BOYFRIENDS

Puberty gives a big push to teenagers to move on from their family. As their bodies mature, so they become naturally attracted to the opposite sex, and longings for intimacy and the pleasures and comfort of touch are transferred from the family to the outside world. The search for a 'mate' is on. This process is very important if successful partnerships are going to be formed later on in life: 'For this reason a man will leave his father and mother and be united to his wife' (Genesis 2:24, NIV).

HIGHER EDUCATION

Going away to college can be a help in making the break from family life. College often means periods away from home and vacations at home, so everyone can get used to the new state of affairs gradually. College also offers a new, self-contained life away from the family, where the young person can experiment at being more independent, with some help still available if necessary.

HOBBIES AND CAUSES

It is in the teenage years that people often start to be consumed by some hobby, interest or cause. For example, it is at this age that sporting ability may become the focus of someone's life as they try to reach the highest level they are capable of, or their support for a 'cause' such as Greenpeace or CND leads them to join demonstrations and get seriously involved. Such interests outside the family can provide a source of meaning and a goal to aim for, and also an outlet for energy, enthusiasm and even care for others—all things which in the past the family might have provided in different ways.

CAREER

In much the same way as college or personal interests, a young person's career choice can help them to establish their separate life from their parents. A job usually brings with it increased financial independence. The workplace is a whole new world to the young person, where they are hopefully seen as an adult from the outset, a world where they stand or fall on their own effort and ability, and where they are not so-and-so's son or little sister, but a person in their own right.

**XERCISE**

Now have a quick look at your two pen-portraits again and (yes, you've guessed it!) try to find which things these young people are using as stepping-stones to help them in their separation from their family. For example, 'Sarah':

◆ *Peer friendship groups.* Sarah has a best friend of long standing, with whom she confides most things—this relationship is probably replacing her reliance on her mum for support.

◆ *Youth culture.* Sarah listens to mainstream music, and dresses with the fashions. She buys these tapes and clothes herself, and they do express that she affiliates herself more and more with people her own age than with her family.

◆ *Boyfriends.* Sarah has had a number of relationships, not all positive by any means. However, she does seem to get a lot of confidence from these relationships, as well as her needs for affirmation, excitement, fun and physical comfort. She is sometimes the one who calls things off, giving her a sense of independence. These relationships may be helping to replace her reliance on her (absent) father for such emotional needs.

◆ *Higher education.* This is not an option open to her.

◆ *Hobbies/causes.* These are not her scene at all.

◆ *Career.* She seems to have rather unrealistic ideas as to what jobs may be open to her, but aspires for things which are outside of her family's world, for example working as a translator.

Spend five or so minutes writing your thoughts about each of your young people, and compare them to Sarah. You may find other things which I haven't listed which they are using as stepping-stones.

FEEDBACK

All of these stepping-stones can be positive stages on the way towards adulthood. However, they can also be negative influences in the lives of young people. The peer group may lead into teenage activities such as using drugs or involvement in crime. Youth culture can take extreme and worrying forms such as the racism of skinheads. Girlfriend/boyfriend relationships can degenerate into the empty comfort of sex. Higher education can be an escape from the outside world rather than a move towards it. Hobbies and causes can become all-consuming and isolating. Careers can be disappointing, demeaning and depressing.

It is sad, but true, that a young person's ability to use these stepping-stones of adolescence positively will depend on the quality of care they have received as they have been growing up. These represent their first hesitant steps towards taking care of themselves, and they have only their previous experiences to go on, only their family life as a model to emulate. For example, Sarah takes her memories of her father's care for her, and her father's relationship with her mum, into her relationships with boyfriends. This affects her expectations.

This is where the inside world of growing up and the outside world interact. Many issues that are commonly seen as 'teenage problems' such as drugs, gang violence, sex, eating disorders and so on, may in fact be symptoms of a teenager's struggle to come to terms with this process of growing up and moving on from home—whatever that home life has been like. We will be looking at these things in more depth in chapter 7.

Thinking about these issues also brings us back to where we started at the beginning of this chapter, and how an individual's history, their life until now, will affect their ability to cope with adolescence and adulthood beyond. But this is the end of our study of the inside world. Time to go out and celebrate the end of another chapter—you've worked hard, well done!

4 TELLING THE GOOD NEWS

Jude Levermore

INTRODUCTION

For me this is it. What I mean is, this is what it's all about isn't it? The nub of the issue, where the rubber hits the road; the thing we all want to do, tell young people the good news. This chapter will help you to do just that. The idea is that we'll explore together what the good news is and then I'll share some practical tips in doing it.

WHAT IS THE GOOD NEWS?

INSTRUCTIONS

This section will require you to think about your own coming to faith. You may need your Bible to hand. You will also need to find someone with whom you can talk about the experience of conversion. This special someone needs to be a Christian, with a story they can tell of how God met and changed them. It doesn't have to be dramatic, but they need to be someone who is happy to talk about it, not necessarily someone used to giving their testimony. You will need to interview them for the exercise at the end, so now would be a good time to arrange a meeting time with them.

 INPUT

'What is evangelism? It's people who know the good news about Jesus telling other people who don't.' So say Moser, Stewart and Vaughan, in their book *No Guts, No Glory*, about youthwork. What they don't go on to look at is what that good news might be—and if you don't know what it is how the heck can you tell it?

The good news, or 'godspel' in Old English, is a translation of the Greek word *evangelion*, where we get our word evangelism from, but none of these helpful little facts can help us really to understand what it might be. My theory is like this: there is the good news as set out in the Bible—that is the story of Jesus Christ related in the Gospels (there's that word again); there is the good news as each of us as Christians have experienced it, and there is the good news in relation to what God might want to do for and with young people. Each of these is good news, and each is separate but related. Think of it like this: the Bible tells us of the good news for us, we experience it, we tell young people about it.

'Fine,' you say, 'but you still haven't

distilled out exactly what it is!' Many guides to evangelism assume either that you know what the good news is or that it can be summed up in a few sentences. They will write it out for you as an ABC, or as some kind of formula—first you tell them they've sinned, then that because of that there is a gap between them and God, then that Jesus died to bridge that gap, to restore the relationship, then you tell them that if they repent of their sins and believe what you've just told them they will be saved. The idea of telling the good news, they say, is to learn how to present these ideas clearly. I don't want to appear flippant or arrogant, but I disagree. I believe the good news to be about a relationship—a relationship with the living God. Now, as with all relationships, this doesn't follow a nice simple pattern, neither can it be reduced to a formula. 'Yes, but you've got to start somewhere,' I hear you cry (probably desperately by now). Well, you are right, you do, and I would suggest you start with relationship, and that that relationship starts with you. Maybe it's easier to start out from another angle.

How did you become a Christian? Was it:

(a) reading a Bible

(b) hearing God speak to you

(c) feeling the sudden need to attend church or

(d) having someone come alongside you and explain things to you, take you to a meeting, or show you how to read your Bible.

I'll bet for most people reading this it was (d). If it wasn't, you've scuppered my plan!

My point is that God became a human being, entered relationships. He *became* the Message, the Word made flesh—that is the good news—and we enter relationships with others in order to convey that, and it is that relationship which becomes good news to the young person. As such, it is we ourselves who become the message in the same way as Jesus did for us. We are to be the good news, as Jesus is good news to us. Formulas may be hooks upon which to hang things, but in the end they are useless. We are the message Jesus sends to young people. Good news.

This isn't just something I thought up, it's what Jesus said in what's called 'the Great Commission' at the end of Matthew's Gospel, 'Go, and make disciples of all nations . . .' is what Jesus says. He doesn't tell us what to say. There is no three-point plan. But we are not to convert people, but to make disciples of them. Jesus said, 'I am the way, the truth, and the life, no one comes to the Father except through me' (famous, and favourite bits of the Bible can sometimes seem over-used, but bear with me). Jesus didn't say, 'This formula must be followed if you want to become a Christian, first you do (a), then you think (b), and finally you believe (c), and then that's it, you have eternal life!' Jesus offers relationship. Jesus offers to meet us and change us. How he does that is up to him.

EXERCISE

Spend about twenty minutes with a piece of paper and a pencil thinking about how you came to faith in Christ. Think about it in terms of how Jesus met you and changed you. You might want to start a long way before you made that final decision, and look at how God was at work before you knew him, or you may want to start with the decision and look at how that coming to faith has changed you. Either way, jot down what happened in the form of notes.

Now I want you to find that special someone I mentioned earlier. What you need to do is to get them to do the

same as you have just done, but out loud to you, so that you can put it down in note form like yours. Be careful not to put words in their mouth, or to compare your experience with theirs at this stage. What I'm asking you to do is to interview them about how Jesus has met them and changed them. It will probably take you a bit longer to record theirs than it did to write up yours, so give yourself an hour to talk to them and write the notes.

With all this complete you now have notes on how two people were influenced by a relationship that Jesus offered them. Now is the time to look and see how they compare. Is there any common ground between how Jesus dealt with the two of you? Write up your findings—take about a page of A4 to do it and give yourself a quiet half an hour to complete it properly.

EEDBACK

When you look at the variety of ways Jesus met people, as described in the Gospels, the differences are astounding. Knowing this, I would not be surprised if there was no common ground at all in your experiences. However, as both of you are likely to be from the same church and a similar background, it could be that you have described something fairly similar. If this is the case can I ask whether this is because the experience is similar or is it because the language you describe it in is the same? Let me expand on that. As Christians we become embedded fairly fast in a Christian sub-culture that says that to be a Christian you must have confessed your sins, experienced God's forgiveness and been filled with the Holy Spirit, more or less in that order. This means that we tend to interpret our experiences in

the light of this. So, say one person felt God particularly as a presence with them in a room when a worship time was happening, and felt that God was comforting them, and this feeling was powerful enough to make them cry, and another felt a strong urge to find out about this Jesus and so read their Bible, and when they came to the part, 'and the Word became flesh and dwelt among us', felt a strong conviction that, yes, indeed this was true. Now these two experiences, different though they are, could be interpreted as God convicting the person of their sin. That may not be the full story, but if that's what everyone tells you should happen first, then that will be how you interpret it. I hope that I've explained that OK. Of course it may be that you both did have a similar encounter with Christ, but look back at the two accounts and when you take away any Christian jargon that might be there, are the conclusions you come to about the similarities and differences changed in any way? By the way, just to let you know, the two accounts that I've described are real-life experiences, I didn't make them up.

It may be helpful to look at the Gospels themselves to back up what I've said here. You see Jesus meets lots of people during his ministry, and seems to deal with them in many different ways. Take the story of Jesus' encounter with the rich young ruler (Luke 18:18–30). This could be said to follow the kind of pattern that I've said church sub-culture would seem to foster. In other words Jesus challenges the man with his actions, shows how they still fall short of God's standards, and then offers hope of salvation if the man repents and turns from his current course. It might be more difficult for a camel to go through the eye of a needle than for him to enter the kingdom of God, but with God all things are possible. This way of dealing with people is miles away from the way Jesus dealt with the sick—look at the woman with bleeding for twelve years, for example (Mark 5:25–34). Here is a woman who has suffered greatly, she has tried everything, is at the end of her tether. Jesus offers her healing and acceptance. There is no call to repentance, no threat of hell, only peace and freedom from suffering. No action is required on her part but to reach out. I could go on, but I won't! With example after example of the difference Jesus made to the people he met, and still each would be individual, there seems to be no overall pattern. Jesus didn't work to a formula. He offered himself. Our job is to allow Jesus to do that in the lives of young people. We can't control it, or direct how it happens. We need to show young people how they can encounter Jesus, how he can become part of their lives. What happens then is up to him.

▌ TELLING THE STORY

INSTRUCTIONS

For the exercise at the end of this section you'll need to do some research that may involve a trip to the library. If that kind of outing requires some organizing from you, then you may want to think about when you can fit it in. It would probably be good to sort it out now rather than get to that part and grind to a halt because you can't fit in a trip to the library for three weeks!

NPUT

Jesus offers relationship, we've established that. Our job is to allow young people to find out about this relationship, we've established that. The question now is how to go about doing that. The story of Jesus is recorded in the Gospels, and it's this story that young people need to hear. You could put it in a nutshell like this: God the Father loved us who he made so much that he sent his Son, a human being, to die on a cross, to rise after three days, to conquer death, and to reconcile us to himself, so that, when we recognize all that, we can share in a new life with him. However, telling that story, powerful as it is, is not all there is to say. Jesus is not about dry facts, but about a living relationship, so how do you put that across?

I guess the answer is in a multitude of ways, which I have catagorized into three sections.

◆ Modelling

◆ Contextualizing

◆ Experiencing

So let's look at each one in turn.

MODELLING

Young people meet us first. It's the quality of the relationship that young people have with us that's important to them, at least to start with. Our friendship is key to them and, as such, its depth and sincerity are vital. The reason that they are so key is that this is how the young people first meet Jesus. Jesus is present by his Spirit in his people. He is no longer present in a human body, nor in the Holy of Holies in the temple, but God is present now in his people. 'We know that we live in him and he in us, because he has given us of his Spirit. And we have seen and testify that the Father has sent his Son to be the Saviour of the world. If anyone acknowledges that Jesus is the Son of God, God lives in him and he in God. And so we know and rely on the love God has for us' (1 John 4:13–16, NIV). In meeting us, young people meet Jesus. Frightening, isn't it! This just goes to show how careful we must be of these friendships—they are precious things to God. God's love is unconditional, our love is partial. We love best those who love us, who conform to our standards. Young people often don't give back, their standards are very different to ours. But we are called to love them whatever, whether they are interested in our faith or not.

I find that hard. It is easy to love those young people who make a change, who meet Jesus and alter, who are eager disciples. I get excited about people like that. It is harder to keep up with young people who have rejected God, who still value my friendship, want that love, but somehow can't bring themselves to respond to it. Perseverance pays—you might not know when, but those seeds of care, concern and the love of God may well bear fruit much later when we are out of the picture. A minister I know says that many of the young families who come to faith after having their children baptized speak of a youth leader or Sunday school teacher, who influenced them, but whose name and details they can't now remember! Young people test what we say by our actions. American writers on youth ministry talk about 'earning the right' to talk to young people about Jesus, but my feeling is that it goes further than that.

Actions speak louder than words, and our actions and words need to be congruent (I thought I'd put that big word in just to make me look clever, no, really, I think it sums up the idea best, I suppose I mean that they need to bear each other out). In other words it's no good saying that Jesus accepts us as we are, that he died for us while we

were still sinners, if we then don't allow young people who are stealing from the local shop to be close friends with us. What I mean is our words and actions must match. There's another aspect to this modelling too. Do you remember in the first section of this chapter I talked about 'the Great Commission' in Matthew 28:19, 'Go and make disciples of all nations'? Well in John's Gospel, the Commission is the same but this version also tells us how to go, 'As the Father has sent me, I am sending you' (John 20:21, NIV). So we are to go as Jesus went, in other words we are to go in humility, not guns blazing with glory, we are to go in weakness not in power, and we are to go with love, service, sensitivity and suffering. I have heard it said that if you want to know what God is like you look at Jesus. Well in a real sense if you want to know what Jesus is like you should be able to look at Christians.

Now look at me, ducklings. I'm your mother. I'm a duck. Ducks swim.

CONTEXTUALIZING

This is a complicated word for a simple process. We have a context, a time in history that is ours, a setting in the world, a culture. I, for example, am English, from the twentieth century, middle class, white, married, and so on. The gospel (in terms of the written Gospels) also has a context. They were written in the first century, set in a Graeco-Roman culture, the story centring on Israel. Contextualizing is about bringing those two contexts together. It is not about putting the Bible into modern English, that is a common misapprehension. It is vital if we are faithfully to tell the story of Jesus that we first understand it, and that means first of all getting to grips with the original context.

You see, if you don't understand that the shepherds in the nativity story were a kind of underclass, that in that point in history they weren't allowed into places of worship, that their evidence was not admissible in court and so on, you miss an important part of the Christmas message—that Jesus came for the poor, the outcasts, those on the edges of society, that they are the ones God chose to be central to his plan. It's no good just translating shepherds for farm workers and expecting people to get the total point God was making. We need to work at understanding the context of the Gospels. But of course we need to work at things the other way around too. As I mentioned in chapter 2, young people have their own language, their own value system and codes. Those need to be clear to us too in order for us to begin to make connections between the two worlds. We are not always going to get those connections right but we need to be making them, tentatively, and more importantly we need to be encouraging young people to make them for themselves.

Now look, ducklings, this is water. It's wet like a puddle, but deep, and it's what we swim in.

EXPERIENCING

We have found at Oxford Youth Works that God meets with young people, often in a profound way, when we as youthworkers provide the opportunities for young people to experience him. By this I mean, during times of worship that we have organized, God has touched young people who previously had no knowledge of him. The ideas surrounding young people and worship are obviously covered in depth in chapter 8, but let me just say here that giving young people space, in quiet, to open themselves to God and providing them with a symbol or idea on which to focus has been one of the most valuable evangelistic tools I have ever seen.

Now, ducklings, in you go. This is swimming.

So then, there you have it. You make Jesus known to young people by modelling him, that is by 'being Christ' to the young people you are friends with, by contextualizing, that is by telling the story in a way that makes links between the cultures, and by providing opportunities for young people to meet Jesus. Now I think this may be the point at which I would like to say one very important thing, and that is that with young people from a non-church back-ground you may well have a situation where one of them might say, 'I have met this Jesus and this is what I want,' but they may have no knowledge about him. I have come across one situation where they didn't even know about what happened on the cross, but they had felt the presence of God touch them and wanted to respond. This is powerful stuff. The point is that this first meeting is just that—a first point of contact between Christ and the young person. It is not necessarily a conversion. It is the beginning of a relationship, and if that relationship is to develop it needs to be nurtured, and that nurturing is just as much our responsibility as the initial introduction. Telling the good news to a young person from outside the church's influence is a long slow process. It's about making an introduction, explaining how to make friends, reintroducing, helping the young person to interpret their experience of God, being with them on their faith journey and allowing them to accompany you on yours.

 **XERCISE**

Choose an incident from the Gospels where Jesus meets a single person, an individual, and speaks to them. An example might be the story of Zacchaeus (Luke 19:1–10). Find out everything you can about that story, every little detail and what it might mean. Ask to borrow books about it from your minister, or try your diocesan library, or that at your nearest Bible or theological college. Your local library might help. Write a commentary on that story that looks in depth at the context of the story. Do this thoroughly—the research might take you a couple of hours and the writing another half an hour or so.

Now try to make some links between that story and a group of young people you know. What might strike them as particularly relevant, particularly applicable to their current situation? What aspects might be difficult for them to understand or identify with? Why? Would the story be more appropriate to another type of group and, if so, why? Take half an hour to think about this and jot down some thoughts.

 **EEDBACK**

This kind of contextualizing is hard work, isn't it? Did you find that studying the story in depth helped you to link it to the lives of young people or did it make it even more difficult? I find that this kind of study is extremely helpful to my ministry. It is not the kind of thing I would ever get young people themselves to do, and it is not something, necessarily, that I would share with them. In other words, I wouldn't, having done such a study, then go on to tell them my findings. Young people need to be helped to make their own links, not to accept those made for them. Having done all that work, however, please do not think it wasted because you can't immediately pick it up and put it straight down into a youth programme, or use it in a 'just looking' group. If we take seriously the idea that God is interested in these young people then we need to get excited about how the Bible fits into it. You see, making these links between the world of the Gospels and the world of young people is going to help us to understand how God wants to meet the particular young people we are interested in.

This kind of Bible study may help us to do it. Let me give you an example. Looking at the story of Zacchaeus—now here was a man clearly not living as God intended. Many young people I work with, quite obviously don't live as God wants them to. The story of Zacchaeus is that of a man trying to cheat his way through life. I could make a lot of links between this kind of attitude and some specific young people I know. Now how does Jesus deal with it? Well you would think that a call to repentance might be in order, or at least some gentle rebuking, but no—all Jesus does is to invite himself to Zacchaeus' house. If this is the incident you chose to study then you will know just how significant eating with someone at their house was, it showed how committed Jesus was to his friendship with Zacchaeus. Maybe Jesus is just as committed to the young people you know; maybe he longs to meet them in the same way; maybe it is this meeting that will change their outlook, as Zacchaeus' changed. It could be that this, then, is the way forward for you with your young people. Perhaps not finding ways to show them that drug taking, or stealing, or whatever is not in God's plan, but by being committed to them as Jesus was to Zacchaeus, and by giving them

opportunities to experience that love too. Don't get me wrong, I am not condoning some of the behaviour of young people. What I am saying is that sometimes you need to come at things from a different angle. Jesus didn't say that what Zaccheaus was doing was OK, but he dealt with it differently from the way people expected.

Hopefully this example has shown just how important this kind of study can be to your work. Here at OYW we have found that studying like this in groups is helpful, as it gives you a better perspective. But this kind of contextualizing has helped me on many occasions when I couldn't see a way through with the young people that I was working with, and this type of exercise shows how closely linked the three concepts I talked about are—modelling, contextualizing and experiencing. By contextualizing the story, we can better model Jesus, and we renew our experience of him, and see how our young people might experience him too.

GETTING DOWN TO SPECIFICS

INSTRUCTIONS

This section is a more practical 'how to...' look at telling the good news. So, at the end of it, in the exercise, you will need to produce the outline of a talk. It would be good but not essential to tape record this to help you to evaluate it. If you want to do this you will need access to a tape recorder and a blank tape.

NPUT

At Oxford Youth Works we tend to do our telling of the good news in a fairly structured way. We use a residential

experience with our young people to provide us with the opportunity to do what we term 'proclamation'. It is important to stress that all the young people that we take with us on this holiday are ones that we have known for some time. They come because we have invited them, and the whole thing is a package—the proclamation is integral to it, not an added-on extra. In fact for some young people it is the highlight of their day—when you ask them what they enjoyed most about the holiday they will say, 'Captain's Cabaret', or whatever we have decided to call the 'God Spot' that year. Within the residential experience then we have two main ways of proclamation, the

'God Spot' and a piece of drama we call the 'Broken Heart Sketch'.

First, a look at the 'God Spot' then. I suppose the first thing to say is what it isn't—it isn't a 'Spot'. God is at the centre of all that we do—the idea of building up relationships with young people that are deep and valuable is what the week is about. The idea is that we are as Christ-like in our dealings with each other and with the young people as possible. To that end we get up early every morning to pray together, we serve the young people, so they don't do any getting of meals or clearing up, all the games are ready set up, they just move from one thing to the next with no bother. (In order to do that we have a 'work crew', made up of young people who have been to camp before, and made some kind of commitment, who come back and do all the work!) We sleep in dormitories with our young people so there is no 'them and us' feel, and we are as flexible as possible about discipline, within the confines of safety and other young people's enjoyment. However, all this said, although we try to show Christ in all our activities by our actions, words and demeanour, it is the 'God Spot' that really makes things explicit.

A typical one would go like this: We would start with one of our team coming on as compère, dressed in a silly costume that links with the theme of the week, and, after some kind of jokey warm-up act, they introduce two more team members in even more outrageous costume, sometimes drag, who lead everyone in the singing of some silly songs, old pop songs seem to work the best. They go off, and the compère takes over with some kind of farce, maybe a silly competition, that results in the humiliation of another member of the team, and nearly always involves custard pies or disgusting food combinations! The singing duo come on for one more silly song and then the compère stands up to introduce the speaker, saying, 'Ladies and gentlemen, please give a very warm welcome to . . .' and the final team member involved will come to the front and do a short 'talk'. These talks follow on each night so there is progression through the week, they usually have a Gospel story in them, taken more or less straight from the Good News Bible, which the speaker will have in front of them, and they last no more than five minutes on the first night rising to about ten on the last. So there you have it. At the end the compère will stand and announce the next activity, usually the last one before bed, often some kind of party.

On the last morning of the week we announce an extra special activity, the young people gather in the room where the 'God Spot' is held and unannounced we perform a sketch from America called 'The Broken Heart Sketch'. It stars members of the team in the roles of a young person, Jesus, the devil, a member of the opposite sex to the young person and a parent of the young person. It takes the audience through a young person's life, with divorce, sex, drugs and alcohol, as well as good and evil, all covered. It ends with the young person giving their broken heart to Jesus and being given a new one. It is simple, powerful and takes about twenty minutes to perform, during which you can hear a pin drop! At the end of it we offer small groups to talk about the issues raised. The young people choose which to go to, and each team member goes with young people they know well. The groups are led by volunteers on the team who don't have young people they especially want to go with. This sketch is modelling, contextualizing and experiencing all in one. Drama in this way seems to work very well in getting across the message.

A few hints then on writing a talk, and then an opportunity to do it for yourself.

First, I would say don't try to get in too much. One clear point is all that you need, and certainly all you will be able to get across. So your point might be that Jesus was the Son of God, not just a good man but the Son of God. Everything you say, then, should point people in that direction. You only have between five and ten minutes, so don't waste time on meaningless jokes and introductions. Talking without notes is best, but scary, so notes, if you've got them, need to be minimal, on little cards and only looked at if you forget what comes next. Try to link what you're saying with the experience of the people to whom you're talking. For example, if yesterday you all took part in a game that went disastrously wrong you could link that into your talk like this, 'I suppose God must feel about the world like we felt yesterday about the daft wide game Kenny made us play . . .' You get the idea? Don't forget to contexualize, to bring together the worlds of the young people, and the world of the gospel to show where they meet. Finally, have your last line in your head. It's often the thing people remember about a talk, so make it snappy, make it sum up what you've said and make it relevant to your point. Then deliver it confidently and leave it there.

EXERCISE

Write a talk of between five and ten minutes in length that you could deliver in a setting such as the holiday I've described. When you have finished, record it on tape. Having listened to yourself, grade yourself on the following:

◆ **ability to stick to one point**

◆ **ability to get that one point across to an audience**

◆ **ability to make the message relevant to the particular young people involved**

◆ **ability to tell the Gospel story**

◆ **ability to make it interesting**

◆ **ability to make it understandable**

◆ **ability to create a lasting impression.**

Grade yourself from A–D on each. If you can get someone else to grade you too, this will help you to see how objective you are being.

FEEDBACK

Preparation is the key in giving any talk—not just preparation of the material and your notes, but preparation of yourself. Spending time in prayer on your own with God before you think about your talk's subject is vital. This is God's opportunity to speak through you. He can only do that if given the chance—you need to listen before you speak. Were you impressed at how you did, or do you feel that you could improve? Of course it's always possible to improve, but generally I think anyone should be able to give a talk like this if called upon. There's no doubt about it, some people are especially gifted in this area. They could have been stand-up comedians or policiians if God had not called them to work with young people!

If you are one of those I envy you—the rest of us have to work hard at these skills.

Did your grades and your other markers more or less agree? I tend to find that where people disagree is in whether or not they were understandable. You see, you have been grappling with the material for a while in your preparation, you understand it inside out. It is hard then when you come to finally write up what you will say to come at it from an angle that is fresh. Your audience will have never heard what you are saying before; it is old hat to you, and you might, therefore, gloss over bits that seem obvious to you in their simplicity, but which might be as clear as mud to your audience. Talking of 'old hat' and 'as clear as mud', how was your use of devices like that? They can often be very important in explaining things. I find that I might need to say the same things in several different ways in order to get my point across clearly. Metaphors and similes can really help here—they let you repeat yourself without it sounding like you are stuck in a groove.

How well you know your young people will, of course, affect how well you are able to make the message clear to them. Understanding their context is important— they use words that have different meanings to us; you need to be wary of these. I would suggest that you don't use them unless they sound natural to you. A thirty-five-year-old describing Jesus as a 'well-safe, happening geeser' sounds ridiculous, and will only come over as such, as far as language goes. Be true to yourself is my advice. Of course body language is important too, although it's not going to come over on tape! How you stand is part of the message so it's worth thinking about. Some of the speakers we've had have chosen to sit on a table at the front of their audience, more of a perch really; to my mind this works well. Expressive gestures can help your audience to visualize what you are saying—that's important, you need to engage with your audience, to paint word pictures for them to help them be there when you are telling the story. You are not out to give an intellectual discussion on the theories behind Jesus being God's Son but to help them grasp the truth of it.

One last thing before we move on: this kind of talk must not happen in a vacuum— it must have a context. For my money, the best it can have is while away like this. It needs to be done sensitively, we're not about brainwashing. It needs to be done in the context of a loving, accepting environment that says, 'You're OK, God loves you as you are, now come and hear more.'

▓ THINKING STRATEGICALLY

INSTRUCTIONS

This is the final section in this chapter, so you're nearly there! You just need to read the input here and do some thinking for yourself about how it applies to you and then you will have finished yet another chapter. Well done!

NPUT

As I said at the end of the last section, the proclamation of the good news shouldn't happen in a vacuum. Telling the good news needs to be a strategy that you work to. Working with young people from outside church experience, I have found that you need to build up to a telling of the gospel. You need to begin way before, developing a relationship, and we all know how much work they can take! Then a two-way respect needs to develop, where you listen to their ideas about the world and take them seriously, and begin to share your ideas with them. You need to have been through stuff together, often on overnight trips, residentials and the like, trust needs to form on both sides. Finally the gospel, the truth of the good news, needs to be explained.

I feel very strongly that this last stage should not be rushed, and should not be in the form of 'take it or leave it' or even worse 'take it or leave me'. You see that relationship with you will now be very precious to that young person. To exploit it by saying that you either become a Christian or lose my friendship is wrong, it puts too much pressure, it makes quick converts not long-term disciples. There are people who put a figure to how many times a young person has to hear the gospel before they can understand it and respond. That seems a bit silly to me—each person is obviously different—but for some, coming to faith is a long-term, slow process which we should not hurry along for our convenience. God's time is the right one. That gospel proclamation may have to be done several times and in several ways before the penny drops, but when it does, boy is it worth the wait!

So then let me share with you my strategy for one group of young people with whom I wanted to share my faith.

When this group were in Year 9 at school, in the last term of that year, I first made contact with them and went on a school residential as a helper.

Over that summer holiday I made sure I saw them once or twice around the town.

While they were in Year 10, I increased the time I spent with them, I organized a trip to the swimming pool nearby with a wave machine and then I organized a weekend away at a cottage in Wales.

That Easter I offered them places on the OYW holiday. They went and heard the gospel for the first time.

For the rest of that term I remained close to them, we went up to London together and I spent time with individuals.

Over the summer we did another overnight, where I talked more about God.

They started to come to a weekly meeting in Oxford called 'Worship'.

The next year I offered one a place on work crew.

The rest I kept up with in their jobs and further education.

They are now eighteen and next year four of them will be going to university, one of them now acts as a young leader for OYW, the rest I see at least monthly for a chat and one has started going to church in her village.

My strategy now is to continue my friendship, and to try to get them involved in an alternative worship service that is starting up in our local town.

Now obviously for each group I may work slightly differently, but I plan long term for the young people I am now getting to know in Year 9. It strikes me as irresponsible to start a work with young people and not have a clue where it is going, to say nothing of a waste of time.

EXERCISE

Spend some time now, on your own, thinking about a strategy for the young people you are getting to know. Pray about it and then try in your head to answer the following questions:

◆ **How can I get to know them better?**

◆ **What do I need to put in place to deepen our relationship, to give us memories to share?**

◆ **When will I tell them, in words, the good news?**

◆ **In what context will that be?**

◆ **How can I make sure that they don't just become converts but disciples?**

◆ **When they become disciples, what structure do I need to help them grow in the faith?**

◆ Where does church fit in?

When you've answered those, write out a strategy for reaching your young people, a strategy for telling them the good news.

EEDBACK

If you can get answers to those questions I have set then you are on your way to developing a plan that will see you through several years. Things take time to get established before any 'fruit' can be seen. Some fruit you may never see. The worth of a plan like you have made can often only be seen when you have worked for a while without one! I have tried this! It has cost me much heartache, and has been the cause of much wasted time and effort. For me, prayer is the key. Not only yourself, but get others praying for you, and if you have a plan, share it with them. Prayer will stop you doing it all on your own, it will remind you of God's grace and his Spirit. Prayer will help you to prioritize and it will enable you to keep your perspective. I would say, too, don't be afraid to change your plan if you need to. Build in a review process, have someone you can talk to about it who can see things from the outside. Look at your plan again. Have you built in the three aspects that I keep on about—you know, modelling, contextualizing and experiencing? Are they balanced in your plan? I myself tend to go overboard on the modelling, but I know others that get carried away on other aspects. It is important to achieve a balance, so review your plan if you need to in the light of this.

Another thing to bear in mind is that you may have several groups 'on the go', as it were, at one time. This is only a plan for one of them—each group will need a slightly different plan. Even though you may find a pattern that works, this still means you will have 'dead' patches when things are tough because you don't have much to do, and other times when you are trying to do too much at once. If you can, you need to plan these too. This means not having two groups at the same point in your strategy at once! This way of thinking seems hard at first, but it is not denying God's Spirit—it is helping you to do your very best to do what God has called you to, to tell the good news to young people.

Jesus said, 'As the Father sent me, so I send you . . .'

YOUTH CULTURE

5

Pete Ward

FINDING OUT ABOUT YOUTH CULTURE

INTRODUCTION

Youth culture is a mysterious world to most adults, but as youthworkers we have to be willing to find out about the interests and concerns of the young people we meet. Researching youth culture is important because it helps us to understand young people.

At the end of this section there is an exercise which involves doing some practical research with a group of young people. The material in this section can be read before or after you have done the exercise. I realize that the exercise will take a little setting up, but I hope that in the long run the effort will be worthwhile. Talking to young people themselves and finding out about their world is after all what this course is about.

INPUT

Youth subculture is not so strange, after all it's been with us since the 1950s. Most of us grew up with one form of youth culture or another. If you want to understand young people today then there is no better place to start than with your own experience of being teenagers.

I was teenager in the 1970s—now that's a confession isn't it? At the local

comprehensive school which I attended there were basically three youth sub-cultures operating.

The group that I hung around with generally referred to themselves as 'Hairies'. One problem with this description was that our school insisted on hair which was above the collar at the back and not coming over the ears at the side. Thus the scope for hairyness was somewhat limited.

Having said this we were happy to climb into our flared jeans and cheese-cloth shirts and stroll around the town in our clogs on Saturday afternoons. Music was our chief preoccupation and it was generally described as being 'Heavy' or 'Progressive'.

Flicking through the albums in W.H. Smith's, we would savour such wonders as

Free, Deep Purple and, of course, Led Zeppelin. Being a 'Hairy' was an important thing to us and we proclaimed this fact as much as we could. My old school Bible, which I still use from time to time, has scrawled on the spine in ballpoint pen, 'heavy music'.

There was a friend of mine who sat next to me in geography who was most definitely not a Hairy. His name was Rick and he was a Skinhead. I remember one day he was making notes in his green geography exercise book and I noticed that on his knuckles he had written in pen 'LOVE' and 'HATE'. The neat thing about these two words was that they have four letters each and so they fit with comparatively little difficulty on each hand. Rick was mainly into football and he took great delight in following his team Manchester United.

On Saturdays he would get dressed up in wide baggy jeans with large turn ups, a pair of shiny Dr Martens and a blue jacket. This was topped off with a tartan scarf round his wrists. Rick was not really one for music, but when he did go to a disco he would most often bop to Tamla Motown soul music such as Diana Ross and the Supremes or The Jackson Five.

In my town there were then two main youth sub-cultures, but at my school there were three groups of young people. There were Hairies and Skins (later to become Suedeheads) and then there were the rest. The rest were those young people who didn't align themselves with any group. I would now call them 'straights' because they seemed to reject all the trappings of youth culture.

'The rest' at my school seemed to be the ones who joined the chess club, or were active in the school choir or orchestra. They generally did well in school and one of their number was nearly always chosen to be Head Boy or Head Girl. When I later became a Christian and joined the school CU, I found out that most of my fellow Christians were in this group.

 XERCISE

What was the scene like when you were in your middle to late teens? Take about thirty minutes to travel down memory lane and remember your own adolescence.

Were you part of a group? Think about the musical tastes of your friends and the way you dressed. Don't assume

that because you were not one of the spectacular Punks or Teddy Boys you were not in a group. Those not in a group in general opt out by doing things which make them a group of their own.

Is there something you remember that was extremely important to you as a teenager—for example, a particular group, type of clothes, activity or group of people?

Were you aware of other groups in your town or school? What did these groups wear? Is there anything else you can say about them, such as where they hung out or the kind of music they liked? How did you feel about these other young people?

FEEDBACK

Every adult was once sixteen. The problem is we forget what it was like. Young people have not changed so much in the last ten or twenty years that we can no longer understand them. In fact drawing on my own experience I would say that it's the changes that have happened to me as I have grown older that have created the biggest problems for me in understanding young people today.

Remembering my own teenage years is a way to help me get back in touch with what it was like to be sixteen or seventeen. As youthworkers we need to do this kind of exercise now and again because it helps us to understand what young people we know are going through.

Getting in touch with our own teenage years is very helpful, but if we want to understand young people today then we need to start to talk to them. The next exercise helps you to do just that.

EXERCISE

For this exercise you need to be able to talk to a number of different young people. I realize that this is a difficult exercise to complete, but it is important to talk with young people and find out what they think. If we really want to understand young people then there are very few short cuts.

The aim of this exercise is to interview some young people to find out what kinds of groups they are aware of in their school/local area.

1   Before you meet the young people, sit down and devise a few questions which you want to ask them. These could include:

◆ 'Are there different groups of young people in your local school?'

◆ 'Do these groups have different names?' .

◆ 'What makes these groups what they are: do they dress differently, act differently, live in different places?'

2   Get together with a group of young people and try out your questions on them. You should let the group know a little bit in advance that you are wanting their help with this research and make sure they are OK about you writing down what they say. Some young people talk best in a small group rather than one-to-one. You will have to judge this yourself based on your knowledge of the group.

3   Make notes on what they tell you and write these up as the results of your research.

 **EEDBACK**

You probably found it hard to get down on paper everything that your young people told you, but if the exercise went to plan you should have a good insight into what is going on in youth sub-cultures in your local area.

If your area is anything like Oxford then things have moved on apace since the 1970s. One thing you may have been aware of is that young people in the 1990s don't divide up neatly into simple categories such as Hairies and Skins. The teenage scene is much more diverse at the present moment. Strong groupings may not be so readily identifiable.

Having said this, young people today are in general aware of differences between them. Sometimes this is based on musical taste—some like dance music, others like ragga, some like rock. But more often these divisions are based around activities like skate-boarding or sport or going to raves.

Fashion also plays an important role in young people's lives, and styles are rapidly changing. You may have come across descriptions of what different groups are currently wearing. One thing to bear in mind is that styles of dress are as important to boys as they are to girls.

Where young people hang out is another important distinguishing feature in their social activity. Some might spend most of their time at home, while others might be on the street or in the shopping arcade. One of the interesting things I have observed in my own work in schools is how different groups tend to opt for different types of activity during the lunch periods. For instance currently the large minority of Asian boys at the school I visit go home at lunch time, whilst the sporty types stick around for activities such as basketball or football practice. There is one group that hangs around on the covered steps outside a particular classroom every lunchtime. In these kinds of ways the young people mark themselves out as being different.

THE MEDIA

INTRODUCTION

The media is extremely important to young people. Whether it be CDs and tapes, magazines, videos, computer games or the radio, the media is a vital part of most teenagers' lives.

The effect of the media on young people is a very controversial issue at the moment. Both church people and politicians are regularly to be heard on the TV or the radio calling for strong measures to stop the spread of media excesses in violence or sexual explicitness.

Given that the media is so important to young people it is right that we take the time to look at it in some detail. This section is based on two exercises. These exercises require you to do some preparation.

This is an advance warning!

Before you go any further in this section you should have:

◆ purchased three teenage magazines

◆ watched (and, ideally, videoed) *Top of the Pops*.

For the full details see the next two exercises.

EXERCISE

This exercise should take just over an hour.

To complete this exercise you will need to have got hold of at least three magazines that are currently on sale to young people.

It is worth getting a cross-section of these magazines to compare the styles and content. I would suggest you get *Smash Hits* for the younger teenagers, *Just Seventeen* for older girls and *Kerrang!* for boys who are into heavy metal.

Read each of the magazines asking these questions:

◆ **How much of the magazine is designed to sell something to you?**

◆ **What are the main ideas/values you pick up from this magazine?**

FEEDBACK

Teenage magazines, in fact magazines in general, are primarily concerned with marketing products. *Smash Hits* in this sense is little different from the *The Mail on Sunday*—both are financed by and exist to:

◆ entertain us

◆ sell things to us.

The beguiling thing about magazines is that even when they are supposedly entertaining us—for example, interviewing a pop star—they are in fact advertising something. The pop star is usually being interviewed because he has a new record out that week. This is sold to us as news or as a story of

personal interest. It really doesn't matter whether it is found in *Mizz* or in *The Mail on Sunday*. The fact remains that this kind of article is promotion.

Most of the articles are designed to raise our interest in the consumer items which we are being offered. What we need to realize is that young people's magazines are no different from those which we adults read. Youth culture merely reflects adult culture in this respect. What is perhaps different about young people is that they have grown up with advertising and they may be more able to cope with it than we adults.

Teenage magazines are nearly always in one way or another about sex. Specific attitudes will be expressed in the advice pages and in the articles, but there is also a general 'sexual' feel given to the pictures in the articles and the adverts. Once again before we get too judgmental about these magazines we should perhaps take another look at our own Sunday papers. Sex is a constant theme in adult and teenage life.

EXERCISE

Set aside half an hour on a Thursday evening to watch *Top of the Pops* (*TOTP*). It is a good idea to video the programme, if you can, so you can play it several times. Things move fast on this kind of pop show and you may miss out with just one viewing.

When I tried this exercise at home I noticed that there were about seven songs played that evening. In addition there was a run-down of the charts with bits of songs played. For this exercise you need to concentrate on the seven or eight songs which are played in their entirety on the show.

Make notes on each of these areas for each one of the songs.

1   **Describe the clothes the band are wearing.**

2   **Describe the music.**

3   **Give a rough idea of what the song is about.**

When you have completed these notes answer these questions:

1   **How many different musical styles were evident on the show?**

2   **How many different styles of dress were on display and what was the relationship between musical styles and dress?**

3   **What kinds of young people might be interested in each of the different songs? Can you pick out any recurring themes in the lyrics and the images on the videos?**

 **EEDBACK**

1 and 2   When I did this exercise I was amazed at how many different musical styles and types of dress were contained in one programme aimed at young people. Youth culture is tremendously varied and full of innovation at the present moment. Even within one group on stage you can see a wide variety of styles of dress. Youth culture in the 1990s is a great deal more diverse than it was when I was a teenager.

Part of the reason for this is the sheer amount of consumer choice there is available nowadays. Another reason is that the traditional structures or divisions in our society between working class and middle class are becoming more blurred.

3   What is fairly clear from *TOTP* is that there are a great many different groups of young people who are buying these different kinds of music. There is no such thing as 'youth culture'. What is very clear from this television show is that young people are divided into a number of different sub-cultures. Another feature of *TOTP* is the fact that pop music is also being bought by people in their thirties and in their forties.

As a volunteer youthworker there are important lessons to be learned from watching shows like *TOTP*.

First: You cannot assume anything about the likes or dislikes of young people in your local area. Generalizations about youth culture are nearly always wrong.

Secondly: There is no substitute for getting to know a group of young people well and letting them inform us about what they are into.

Thirdly: Youthwork, and especially youth worship, will never appeal to every group of young people. What is good for one group will often be a red rag to the others.

WHERE DOES YOUTH CULTURE COME FROM?

INTRODUCTION

Youth culture is a hot potato in Christian circles at the moment. Some people say that youth culture is leading young people astray whilst others see youth culture as an exciting and new source of energy to renew the church. As a youthworker you need to decide what your attitude is going to be to youth culture. Is youth culture a bad influence on young people or is it a force which can be used for good?

To answer this question I believe you first need to wrestle with where youth culture comes from. What I mean by this is: Who creates youth culture? Is youth culture the invention of adults who are primarily concerned with selling things to the teenage market or is youth culture created by young people themselves?

EXERCISE

What do you think? Is youth culture just the creation of adults who want to exploit young people or do you think that young people create their own cultures using the media as building blocks? Give your opinion in a short written piece not more than 300 words long. You should take about one hour to complete this exercise.

FEEDBACK

Here are two different answers to this question. The first answer is taken from the American book *Dancing in the Dark*. This book is written by a group of Christian college lecturers who got together for a year to study youth culture. In *Dancing in the Dark* the authors argue that young people today are being manipulated by massive powerful multi-media businesses which market music, fashion and images to young people.

Contemporary society merely exacerbates the patterns of generational conflict begun long ago. To put it more strongly and more critically, more and more adults are very much in the business of giving youth the means to show how different they are from older people. In the past, youth typically had to 'generate' their own values, beliefs, and practices. Now, however, corporate North America has found that encouraging relatively distinct generational groups helps the proverbial bottom line. Since youth like to be different, these corporations have decided to heighten that sense of distinctiveness. Why not sell them their 'own' music, clothing, films, TV shows, radio stations— whatever subgroup product the youth market will buy?

Dancing in the Dark, **page 3**

A contrasting view to this comes from the sociologist Paul Willis who argues that young people use the media to create meaning for themselves. They do this by using the symbols offered by the media— for example, hairstyles, items of clothing or ways of speaking—to create their own particular style. Youth sub-cultures come about because of young people making choices about what they wear or what they listen to or how they spend their leisure time. The media is important to these choices, but this does not mean that the young people are not being creative in choosing between the different images being offered to them.

Most young people's lives are not involved with the arts and yet are actually full of expressions, signs and symbols through which individuals and groups seek creatively to establish their presence, identity and meaning.

We are thinking of the extraordinary symbolic creativity of the multitude of ways in which young people use, humanize, decorate and invest with meanings their common immediate life spaces and social practices—personal styles and choices of clothes; selective and active use of music, TV, magazines; decoration of bedrooms; the rituals of romance and subcultural styles; the style, banter and drama of friendship groups; music making and dance. Nor are these pursuits and activities trivial or inconsequential. In conditions of late modernization and the widespread crisis of cultural values they can be crucial to the creation and sustenance of individual and group identities, even to cultural survival of identity itself.

Common Culture, pages 1–2

INPUT

My own feeling is that both of these books have a point. Of course we are all affected by the media and we all use the media in

constructing our own style. If the papers hadn't told us about Pavarotti then most people probably wouldn't have bought the CD. This seems obvious. But not many of us would want to argue that we are all manipulated into liking Pavarotti by the advertising in the papers. This would be to insult our intelligence. The papers have shown us a product which we have decided to buy. It is the fact that we have made a free choice in this matter, based on the obvious merits of Pavarotti, which makes us feel that we are not being manipulated. The argument of *Dancing in the Dark* relies on essentially devaluing this process of decision making. Adults who get upset about the media and young people tend to say that young people are in some way more susceptible to being manipulated. This seems to me to be a bit naïve.

My own feeling is that many Christians are attacking the media because the media offers to young people a different set of choices than those currently operating in the church. In other words the Christians recognize in the media a competitor. The media opens up the world to young people but the Christians want to keep the young people attached to the church. The problem therefore to my mind is not so much the media, it is the closed horizons of the church.

The question of where youth culture comes from is also very important when it comes to alternative worship for young people. If we think that youth culture is essentially a corrupting influence on young people then we will want to create a safe Christian alternative which can be used in worship. If however we recognize that young people are in part involved in the creation of youth culture then it will be natural for us to want to include some aspects of youth culture in worship.

To say that young people create youth culture does not mean, however, that everything they come up with is good. A Christian response to youth culture will affirm the creativity whilst being critical of some aspects which we would want to challenge from a gospel perspective—for example, violence or drug taking.

DEFINING YOUTH CULTURE

INTRODUCTION

As a youthworker I have always been anxious to try to learn as much about young people and youth culture as I can. I realize that in the last resort there is no substitute for spending time with young people and getting to know them well. However at times I have wanted to get a deeper understanding of what is really behind their styles of dress and behaviour. Sociologists have been studying youth culture for a good while now and their work has helped me to understand the young people I work with.

In this section I want to outline three sociological theories about young people. I think it is important to connect theories to real-life situations. I want to use my own youthwork as an example. After an outline of each theory, I will talk about a group of young people that I have come to know over the last few years.

When you have seen my use of the theory, I then give a short exercise in which you can apply the theory to your own youthwork.

NPUT

First, let me introduce the group I am going to talk about. The group are all boys and they are into 'heavy metal' music. Most play musical instruments and they call themselves 'The DEAD'. Along with the music they have nearly all adopted heavy metal styles of dress with long hair, jeans and T-shirts advertising heavy metal bands.

THEORY 1: YOUTH CULTURE IS ONLY NATURAL

You are probably familiar with the saying, 'It's just a stage he's going through.' One of the most important approaches to youth culture could be summed up with this common saying.

From Generation to Generation by S.N. Eisenstadt published in 1956 made the point that young people had to go through a process before they were considered to be adult. This process is most commonly labelled 'socialization'. To be adult in our society means that we know certain ways of behaving, values and moral rules. Young people therefore need to successfully learn how to be adults.

Eisenstadt pointed out that in modern industrial societies there was a growing gap between the world of the child and that of the adult. This gap was a kind of limbo period where the necessary skills and abilities needed for adult life in a modern technological society were acquired. Thus the period young people spend in education has slowly expanded as the demands of industry for more qualified workers have steadily increased. Adolescence therefore is a period of transition between childhood and adulthood.

Eisenstadt points out that whilst making this transition from childhood to adolescence young people band together for support. These teenage groups are a half way house between the world of being a child and the world of being an adult. In these groups young people can help each other by providing a place where advice and knowledge is shared, or just being someone who listens and understands. One example of this is the way that young girls may spend hours discussing boys. The point of many of these discussions is that they give a chance for the young people to test out what is acceptable behaviour in the complex world of sexual relationships.

The groups can also be used as a way of taking risks with other people. An example of this is the way that young people often show up at events in a gang. This can feel threatening to adults but it is much more understandable when we realize that the peer group is one way of approaching situations with the safety of numbers. Often the first question young people ask you when you suggest going somewhere is, 'Who's going?'.

So according to this view, youth culture

serves an important function for modern society because it is the means that young people themselves have developed to help them pass from childhood to adolescence.

APPLICATION

This theory has helped me to see that my friends in the band are involved in music not just because they happen to like heavy metal. The band is so important to these boys because of the close alliances and friendships that come from playing music together and sharing a common image. The sense of belonging is a necessary support in their everyday lives. Within the one band there are smaller friendship groups but within these they are able to share with each other the day-to-day struggles of being a young boy growing up as a 'Mettler'. Being in a band gives them a sense of identity which helps them with the other issues in their life, for example sex or school work.

It is tough to be a teenage boy, but the comradeship of being into heavy metal is one way of dealing with this situation. The lads have chosen this style themselves because it gives them a group identity which helps them to wrestle with the challenge of growing into adulthood.

XERCISE

Choose a group of young people that you know and take about fifteen minutes to make notes on the following question:

In what ways does the group help these young people to grow up?

THEORY 2: SUB-CULTURE—A QUESTION OF CLASS

From your own study so far you will have realized that there is really no such thing as 'youth culture'. What actually exists in any one area or city is a large number of different youth 'sub-cultures'. The idea of 'sub-culture' amongst young people was explored in some depth by a group of sociologists based at Birmingham University in the 1970s. In 1976 they published a collection of essays under the title *Resistance Through Rituals*. The basic argument of this book is that British society is divided by class. The various youth cultures need to be seen in this light. In a series of studies of Mods, Rastas, Skinheads and Teds the link between these groups and working-class communities was established.

The book argues that sub-cultures act as places where young people can create 'cultural' space for themselves over and against the dominant middle-class culture. Thus the origin of skinhead culture was the response of working-class young people to the dual threats of new immigrant populations (thus the racism of skinheads) and the problems of unemployment in the inner cities (thus the adoption of traditional working-class clothes, for example the Dr Marten boot). From this perspective youth sub-cultures can be seen as a set of rituals which are designed to show in a symbolic way the stresses experienced by working-class young people in modern society.

In present-day Oxford the practice of 'hotting' or 'joyriding' can be, to some extent, explained in this way. Over the last four or five years 'joyriding' has attracted to it a number of ritual elements. One of these is the practice of the display, where the stolen car is paraded on the local estate and crowds have come out to see the young people put the car through its paces. There is however a symbolic element to this practice. The main place in Oxford where this kind of behaviour grew up was an estate right next to the Rover car works. The fact that the works have been taking on fewer and fewer people has meant that young people in that area can no longer be sure of a job. Unemployment does not excuse such wanton destruction of other people's property but we should recognize that there is more to this kind of behaviour than just vandalism.

The authors of *Resistance Through Rituals* point us to the fact that the different behaviours, musical tastes and styles of dress which make up youth sub-cultures are essentially class related. Young people in creating these sub-cultures are making symbolic statements about modern-day life. It is extremely important to realize that a young person growing up on a working-class estate will experience life very differently from an Asian young person living over a corner shop or a middle-class young person whose parents both went to university. The diversity of youth sub-cultures find their variety in the basic differences in lifestyle which these situations represent.

APPLICATION

When I looked into the background of the young people in the band I noticed that for most of them their parents were lower middle class. In some cases their parents had made this jump within their lifetime. They may have bought their own home or been promoted in their work from being a manual worker to being a foreman or office worker. In the local school those boys into heavy metal are by no means the majority. The school has a large working-class population, and from these boys the heavy metal kids get a good deal of taunting and abuse. They are called names and given a hard time almost every lunchtime. The heavy metal style to my mind is linked with the change in class status in their families. The abuse in school is explained in the fact that these young people, who invariably will do well academically and go on to higher education, are seen as being different by the rest of the school. The fact that they play music is one way of asserting their identity over and against the rest of the school. Heavy metal music is arguably the most ritualistic of pop music styles.

XERCISE

Again using the group that you have chosen as an example take fifteen minutes to make notes on the following question:

What role does class or race play in the friendships and style of your group?

THEORY 3: SHOCK TACTICS

One of the authors of *Resistance Through Rituals* was Dick Hebdige. In 1979 he published his own book called *Subculture: the Meaning of Style*. Central to this book is the idea that young people in creating sub-cultures are setting out to shock. One of the chief means that they use to do this is by the choice of the things that they wear.

When the punks first appeared on our streets they were a very disturbing sight indeed. It was not just the haircuts. The choice of 'bondage trousers'—until now only associated with sexual deviance—the safety pin through the nose and the bin liner were a symbolic assault on the senses. The message that we are 'trash' was echoed in lyrics like 'No future for you and me' sung by groups like the Sex Pistols.

dance to Tamla Motown music. Middle-class young people in Britian have also been influenced by the music and dress of black people. One example of this is the growing of hair into dreadlocks. At first this was a style adopted by young black people who were into Rastafarian religion and reggae music. In recent times white young people who have become known as 'travellers' have also started to grow their hair in this way. Hebdige argues that youth culture has always been characterized by white young people adopting black style. One of the effects of this is that white middle-class people are shocked by the way young people look.

One of the main ways that young people have created new styles is to take fashion items from different ages and places and combine them to make something new. The Teddy boy owes his name to the 'Edwardian suit' originally all the rage with upper-class young bucks in the 1950s. Teddy boys, however were generally working-class young people. The appropriation of the Edwardian suit and combination with the lace tie which was reminiscent of the bad guy in American cowboy movies created a new style. In the mid 1980s, upper-class young people commonly wore waxed jackets of the country outdoor-sport type. I noticed that within a short period the roughest and toughest working-class young people in my local school had started to adopt these jackets for themselves.

The relationship between upper-class dress and working-class youth cultures in Britain is mirrored by the influence that black culture has had on white youth sub-cultures in Britian. I have already mentioned how the skinheads in my home town used to

APPLICATION

The young people in the band are generally seen as being 'bad'. The leather jackets, black T-shirts with lurid slogans on them like 'Mega Death' are designed to convey a bad image. Heavy metal music has become more and more morbid with a whole style growing up called 'death metal'. The point about this type of youth sub-culture is that whilst it looks bad, in many ways it is fairly harmless. As I said, these young people will probably go on to higher education. We need to realize that to look bad is much easier than being bad. The working-class young people in my local school are much more likely to be involved in drugs, crime and violence than the heavy metal group. But the key thing about this style of dress is that it looks menacing. This in some way compensates the group for not being where the real action is—namely joyriding or going to raves. The heavy metal style is an easy way to rebel without risking the chance to get on in life.

EXERCISE

Choose a group of young people you know in your local area that strike you as being shocking. If you can't think of any local young people then choose a group that you have come across through watching TV. Describe the style and behaviour of this group and then take fifteen minutes to make notes on the following question:

What is it about this group that you find shocking?

6 GROUPS AND HOW THEY WORK

Jude Levermore

INTRODUCTION

Being young is about being in a group. It's about belonging and identity. Being young is about friends, and friends go about in groups. No wonder then that youthworkers need to know how groups work. In order to work effectively with young people, a youthworker needs to know how to work effectively with groups. So never fear, here is a chapter all about them! The idea is that it will give you some of the theory behind how groups form, and then give you some ways of working with groups of young people that should help you to deepen your relationships with them, and help you to communicate more effectively. Here goes!

US AND GROUPS

NPUT

Groups are made up of individuals. (I know it's obvious but sometimes it's good to state the obvious!) We are all individuals. We know just how complicated we are, just how many hang-ups and funny personality traits we have. Well a group is made up of individuals like us—a collection of people who don't leave their individuality behind them, but carry it with them into any group to which they belong.

We are all part of many different groups: our family group, our friendship groups, our church groups and so on; both formal groups, like football clubs, and informal ones, like a group who all drink at the same pub; we are in groups, like them or not.

As we all bring ourselves into our groups with us this makes the whole thing very complicated. What people who make theories about groups do is to try to simplify all these complications and draw out some common things that are true for most groups. This is valuable, and I'll be explaining some of the theories to you. But remember, each group is different, it's made up of different individuals. God made each of us unique, we've all had different influences on our lives. We all act differently when we're in a group.

XERCISE

This is an exercise in your imagination. We're going to put together a picture of a group of young people you know. Then you can write it up in your

notebook, and use it to test out the theories that are coming up.

I want you to think of a group of young people that you have contact with, or a group you have known in the past. Picture them in your mind. Think about each individual—you might want to jot down their names on a scrap of paper. Think about something for each one of them that makes them an individual, something that makes them slightly different to the others. It might be that they've got a brace, or wear a particular jacket, or like hip-hop music or something else, anything that makes them stand out. You might want to jot that something down next to, or below their name.

Another imagination exercise now. This time about yourself. I want you to think about a smallish group that you are part of. It might be a pub quiz team, or a Bible study group, or a group of work colleagues. Any small group, except your family, that you are a member of will do, but don't choose one that you have a leadership role in. Picture this group in your mind. Once again jot down names and distinguishing characteristics of each member.

FEEDBACK

You should now have two distinct groups, an adult one of which you are a member and a young people's one of which you may or may not be a member. You will need these two groups for the exercise after the next section so don't loose the bits of paper. Did you find it hard to think of a group in which you take part but are not a leader? This is often so with people in leadership roles in their job or in church—it may suggest something about you that you will discover in the next couple of sections!

INPUT

Group theory says that individuals take on roles that they play out in group situations. This role playing is true of us as well as of young people. The reason we play these 'games' and take on these 'roles' is because, as I said before, we are all individuals and we bring our individuality to our group. We bring our needs to our group.

Everybody has needs. You might have seen a diagram like the one below before. It was devised by a chap called Abraham Maslow (1908–70).

He suggests that everyone has needs but that some are more important than others. For example, physiological needs, by which he means food, shelter, warmth and so on, are more vital than self-esteem needs like people giving you praise or having a job that society values. Maslow argues that unless the needs at the bottom of the pyramid are satisfied then those further up cannot be. So, a hungry person would put food before safety, a well-fed person would put safety before friendship and so on. This idea is true of us as individuals but it is also true of the groups we belong to. A person in a group might have the need to have their self-esteem enhanced by playing in the first team, but it is the group's need to have its self-esteem needs met by winning. The group need and the individual need then come into conflict. It's this kind of tension that group theorists say leads to role playing.

THE ROLES PEOPLE PLAY

What follows is a description of some of the roles that people play in groups. Not each group has one of each type, and the list is not exhaustive. Also some people might play more than one role, or play a different role in different groups. But here they are:

Joker or clown.   This is the person who messes around, who mimics others, makes jokes, keeps everyone laughing. They can be helpful in a group, they dilute tension, stop things being too heavy, or they can be a pain! They can disrupt everything, stop anything serious happening and intimidate others.

Peacemaker.   The one who brings everyone together, who is unhappy about disagreements. This role stops conflict, which can be a blessing or a curse. It's a bit like a group nurse sticking plasters on everyone to make people better.

Dominator.   This is the type of person who has done it all before, who launches into long monologues, who interrupts and won't let others finish. This is the kind of person who finds it hard to listen to others, who can always go one better. I bet we've all done it.

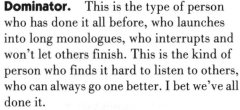

The story-teller.   This role slows down progress as this person goes off at a tangent, they tell stories about themselves and their lives that are unrelated to what is happening now. They can easily hijack a group if they are interesting, or drive people away if they are not!

Now, let me tell you...

The ideas person.   This is the one who proposes a new approach to a problem, the person who can see a new angle, come up with exciting ideas. A person who is dynamic and creative. Beware, they sometimes get carried away.

The passive group member. You've heard of passive smoking, well this is passive group membership. This person doesn't get involved, they withdraw from the group, either by not talking, or by whispering together in corners with other group members. They might sit and doodle, or stare into space. They look bored. Some people just are this way but it can be damaging to the rest of the group if a normally outgoing person suddenly acts like this in a group.

The don. Often found in adult groups here in Oxford this is the kind of group member who puts things on a higher footing, who intellectualizes every discussion, who reads things into what others have said and interprets them for the group. This type of input can be helpful if it is made occasionally. If it is constant others can feel inferior, that they don't need to make an effort, or they might just get plain bored.

Fighter/defender. Hostility can be damaging to a group, physically and emotionally. This type of role is often played by aggressive, defensive types, who feel they are being persecuted or that they are the only one who really cares. They can defend the honour of the weak but often it's themselves they are fighting for.

Helper/facilitator. The encourager of a group, the kind of person who draws others in, who clarifies issues, who keeps open the communication channels, and who makes a group the place you want to be. It would be nice to think this referred to us all but a group made up of people like this would be infuriating, and dull!

So there you have it, we all play different roles within a group. The question is, did you recognize yourself?

EXERCISE

Go back to the groups you thought about earlier, firstly the reference group of young people. Can you identify any of the roles I've just described in that group?

In your notebook make up a table with the person's name, under it the characteristic you chose about them, and under that the role you think they play.

Now try the same thing with the group of which you are a member. Include yourself in this, try to establish as objectively as possible what role or roles you play in this group.

FEEDBACK

The type of role you play in an adult group may well affect what happens when you join a group of young people. Did you find it difficult to match people to roles? Some seem easier to see than others, in my experience, for example, jokers are often quite easy to spot, whereas the ideas person can sometimes be more difficult to identify. Did you find many people with more than one role? This might depend on the size of your group. If you picked a group of four people it is often the case that the participants in a group that size play several roles. A bigger group may mean several people with the same role. Sometimes it seems to me that the descriptions don't quite fit the person I'm thinking of but that they are nearly a 'fighter' or whatever but perhaps not so strongly as the theory describes. Was that true in your groups? Which was easier to see, the adult or young people's group? When I tried it I found that it was not so difficult to label the young

people as it was to do the same to the adults, probably because I could imagine how cross the adults would be if they discovered I was putting them down as a 'storyteller' or whatever!

So, what were you? Were you pleased or horrified with what you discovered about yourself?

EXERCISE

Complete the following sentence, writing a couple of lines about yourself in your notebook:

What I have discovered about myself as a group member is _____

_____.

FEEDBACK

So, you should now have some idea of how you have a tendency to act in a group situation. You may even have some clues as to your motivation for acting this way. But what has it got to do with working with groups of young people? When we enter into the world of young people we enter into their groups, friendship groups, clubs, classes or whatever, and whenever we enter into a group we take on a role. Most of the roles I've described have positive and negative aspects. I hope in completing your sentence you didn't write only in negative or only in positive terms. Most of us have the ability to act for good or bad in the roles we adopt. Looking at them like this helps you to see in which ways you can accentuate the positive and eliminate the negative (as the song goes!). This in turn will help you act for good within the groups in which you find yourself, whether a boring committee or a dynamic youth drama group.

■ HOW GROUPS FORM

INSTRUCTIONS

For this section you will need to go back to the two groups that you used in the last section, so have your notes on them to hand before you start. You will also need to discuss some of what you read next with either one member of your adult group or the whole group. So you need to make sure you can do that, or you'll end up being frustrated!

NPUT

Why groups form is a bit of a mystery, although group theorists would have you believe otherwise! It obviously depends on the type of group as to why it forms. For example the simple answer to the question as to why a football team forms is to play football. However, as with all these things, there is a deeper answer. Remember Maslow's hierarchy of needs? We all have needs that we aim to fulfil—some are basic needs like warmth and others are more complicated like having self-worth. Group theory says that groups form to fulfil these individual needs. Ancient peoples (I don't mean old people but people from a long time ago!) joined together in groups to fulfil their basic needs more effectively. We join groups now because they give us worth, or make us feel good, or because they are the means to an end, like a diploma, that help us to fulfil these higher needs. I bet you thought you went to the pub just to meet your friends—but no, it's to fulfil a higher need!

So, groups form in response to need. However they don't just form and that's it—they go through stages. A group starts when everyone is new, like at the beginning of a

night school class. Imagine the scene: you walk into the classroom and see about ten new faces. By the end of term you will be a group, but right now you don't know anyone, and they don't know you. You begin to talk; someone starts, probably the helper/facilitator role player, and you adopt your role and off you go into the first stage of a new group.

There are lots of people working in the area of group theory who specialize in looking at how groups form, grow and develop. There are lots of theories and lots of models of the process. I have my own theory which is much simpler than most others, and I think it shows the whole thing much more clearly because of it. But then I would, wouldn't I?

JUDE LEVERMORE'S THEORY

Groups change and develop as they get older. In other words, they feel and act differently when they've been together three days to when they've been together three months.

These are the stages I think they go through.

STAGE 1: IS THIS GROUP FOR ME?

This initial stage happens as you first join a group. You find yourself asking the question, 'Do I want to be in this group?' The thing is that everyone else in a new group is asking themselves the same question. This makes the group a place where people are testing things out. Each group member is trying to discover what the rules are, who sets them, what other group members think and so on. In reality it's a sussing out stage. Other group theorists have called this part of a group's development the 'forming' stage (John Adair), or the 'orientation' stage (Roberta Hestenes). It is the first thoughts, feelings and attitudes that a group has.

STAGE 2: THE 'WHERE AM I?' STAGE

This is when status becomes an issue. Imagine it like this: you have been going to a Bible study group for about three months. You feel committed to the group, you go as often as you can, hardly missing any. You feel a part of the group, you belong. The questions that you now begin to ask yourself are, 'How important am I in this group? Am I the leader? Am I the one who knows most about the Bible? Or am I the thick one who everyone tries to help but everyone knows will never quite master the more intellectual challenges?' Hestenes calls this stage 'power and control'. It can be quite an uncomfortable time. Different people may be struggling to head up the group, or to influence its direction. On the other hand no one may want to carry the responsibility that comes from that. It's at this time that leaders emerge, that people leave because they don't like how the group is going, and where group roles are firmly established and become set almost in concrete, so they become nigh on impossible to change. This stage could be described as the 'Am I up or am I down?' stage in terms of status and power.

STAGE 3: THE 'AM I SAFE?' STAGE

Your group is set now—everyone has a role and a level. People know where they stand in the group. If you asked group members to form a line with the group leader at one end and the least important member of the group at the other and all the other group members in between to stand in order of their importance they could do it. The question now is: Would they? Do you see, the level of power of individuals in the group is known, but the question is: Is it safe to talk about it?

You can look at it like this; a lot of things in groups are unspoken and the reason for this is one member is unsure of another's reaction if they were to speak it aloud. For example, if the group said that Joan was the leader, and that Mary was the least important, would Mary cry, and would Mark, Joan's husband, feel upset that he's not considered the leader? It's a minefield, it could upset lots of people, so perhaps it's safer to say nothing about the subject. If a group gets to the end of this stage then it would be safe to talk about this kind of thing. A group that reaches this level is supportive enough to cope with people's hurts and uncertainties. This level of group is rare. Adair calls this stage 'performing' while Hestenes calls it 'trust'.

Most other theorists have at least five stages, some have six or seven! But it seems to me that they can mostly fit into my three, and why make life any more complicated than it is?

So there are three group stages:

◆ Is this group for me?

◆ Where am I in the group?

◆ Am I safe in this group?

XERCISE

Where are the adult group that you thought of? At what stage do you feel they are?

Discuss with another member of the group your feelings about where the group is, or discuss it with the whole

group if you feel it would be more appropriate. Write up your discussion in your notebook.

What would have to happen for your group of young people (the ones you thought of earlier in the chapter) to move to the end of stage three? Write it down in terms of a series of ten points. For example:

1　They would need to learn to listen to each other, especially Kelly who needs to hear that everyone gets fed up with her putting Jo down.

2　They would need to work out if Julie is a member.

And so on . . .

It may be that it would take a great deal more than ten steps to move them to that stage. Well, just write ten that would move them on towards it. On the other hand it might be that you think that they are nearly there, or there already. If this is so then write ten points that you think they must have worked through to get to that stage.

　　The idea is that you come up with ten fairly specific ideas that help to move a group through its stages.

FEEDBACK

It would depend where your group is in terms of the stages as to how difficult or easy the first exercise was, or so I would expect. If your group is in the first stage then the level of 'safety' to talk about things as potentially threatening as this will be low. That is, you may feel uncomfortable talking to another group member about 'where the group is'. It may feel like you are being critical or negative. So how easy or difficult you and your fellow group member found this exercise is in itself an indication of the stage your group is in. If you found it relatively comfortable, and were able to talk to the whole group about it, it seems likely that your group is nearer to the second and third stages. Sometimes it is almost impossible to categorize a group at all. Maybe because different members of the group, as individuals, are themselves at different stages. For example, take a group like this:

Mary, a twenty-four-year-old, confident, computer programmer, who has been in the group since it started, four years ago.

John, a nineteen-year-old unemployed school leaver, who started coming to the group last month.

Harry, a twenty-year-old student, who has been a group member since he met Mary two years ago.

Susan, a twenty-two-year-old nurse, who comes to the group when her shifts allow.

Sam, a twenty-five-year-old teacher in the local school, who moved to the area and joined the group when Harry did.

This group is a dynamic one. In other words it is one with a membership that changes over time. My thoughts were that this group might be the young adults group of a church. Young adults tend to move around a bit and so a group like this is bound to have a changing membership. This means that different individuals feel differently about the group and its stage. Take John—he is most likely to be feeling that he is in the 'Is this group for me?' stage. He is new to the group, less academic, has a lower income and is the youngest. His arrival changes the group, it may bring it from the second stage, 'Where am I?', to the initial stage of 'Is this group for me?' This isn't only because John is asking himself that, but it could also be that his arrival has prompted Mary to ask the same question. She may feel that she is now too old, needs to move on, or that the group, in trying to accommodate John, has become too simple.

So you see, it's not just time that makes a group move through the stages, it's people. And the stages don't just neatly go in order either; groups move through them, forward and backwards.

The second exercise asked you to think in terms of moving a group on. I hope you have come up with ideas that the *group* would have to do, and not things that you would have to do for, or to, the group. It seems to

me that forcing a group to move through the stages before it is ready is very unhelpful. What is useful however is to have a clear idea in your mind as to where the group is and why, and to be able to work out what might happen when a new member joins, or an old one leaves. Perhaps it is worth pointing out that as an adult getting to know young people you are joining their group. This act of joining is therefore a serious one because of the consequences it might have on the group. Your friendship to the group will affect it just by your being there. Being aware of this can be very helpful in that it means that you can make sure the group remains positive by helping the young people to answer the questions of every stage: Is this group for me? Where am I in this group? Am I safe in this group? By not answering the questions but by engineering times when the young people can begin to answer them for themselves, you are helping the group to become supportive to its own members.

GROUP LEADERSHIP

NPUT

We, as adults, are natural leaders. You might not feel like it among your fellow adults, but put in a group of young people, adults take on the leadership role. Nearly always if you take a group of young people and stick an adult in there they become the leader. The aim of this section is in two parts, first, to help you to be a good leader, and secondly, to help you put away your leadership role if that is more appropriate.

Now, do you remember the picture about 'needs' at the very beginning of this chapter? It was of Maslow's hierarchy of needs. I said then that as group members we

bring our needs and our individuality to any group that we're in. Well that is also true of groups that we act as leaders in. If, as leaders, we have a great need for people to show us respect, perhaps because we don't get that from our jobs or families, then our type of leadership will be of a style to get us respect. You see it's like this: if when I'm leading my group is the only time in my life I can get anyone to listen to me, I am going to tend to be the kind of leader who talks too much, is overbearing and tells the group what to do. I am unlikely to be the kind of leader who listens carefully to everyone, who makes sure that each person feels they have been heard, and then lets the individual make up their own mind.

Group theorists have lots to say on this too. They talk about *leadership styles* in the same kind of way as the roles. In other words, they describe different types of leaders. Here are the four most common:

◆ autocratic

◆ authoritative

◆ democratic

◆ laissez-faire.

I've done a little chart below that lists the things that makes each one different.

Autocratic
Controlling, asks, and answers all the questions, determines the aims for the group, group members do as they are told, they are followers. This type of leader is domineering and dictatorial.

Authoritative
Takes strong control, has a plan, but is open to other ideas. Asks the questions, will listen to answers, but may disregard them. Gives support to group members.

Democratic
Shares the control and leadership, allows the group to discuss all policies.

Laissez-faire
Passive type of leader. Minimal control, lets it drift. No form is put onto the group.

This is all very well but it isn't much help to us to decide which style we might have or need to have. All of the styles above look fairly negative—it is easy to pick faults with all of them. I think that it can be described better. I would rather talk about leadership as a continuum—that is to see leadership styles as things that are continuous, not as separate types like the roles idea, but more

of a line stretching from very controlling and autocratic to very free and easy. I would say that leaders can move up and down the line and that they do so because of their own needs and the needs of the group. If I had to draw a chart, mine would look like this:

Autocratic, all controlling	Laissez-faire, no control

This type of idea doesn't say that some kind of leadership is bad and some good, because it needs to take the group, the leader and the situation into account.

Let me give you an example.

In an emergency situation a leader has to take control. If as youthworker you were with a group of young people when there was an accident and one of them was seriously hurt, you would have to order another member of the group to phone for help, instruct another to help you with first aid, tell another what to do with the rest of the group and so on. In other words you would be using an autocratic leadership style. You wouldn't gather the group around and ask them for ideas as to what might be good to do next. You would just order them to do it. This just goes to show that it's not only our needs and the needs of the group that determine a leader's style, it is the external situation.

So although no one style can be said to be good or bad in itself, some are more appropriate than others to different leaders, groups and situations.

XERCISE

What kind of leader are you? Spend about fifteen minutes thinking about all the groups that you have led. Is there a pattern in the kind of leader you are? If you had to mark yourself on the continuum where would you be?

FEEDBACK

Most of us have a natural leadership style, a way of leading that we tend to revert back to if all other things are equal. All the same, most of us can also adapt our leadership to suit the situation. It's this adaptability that is of value to us as youthworkers. We need to be just as able to be autocrats as we do to be diplomats or non-leaders, and most importantly we need to know when each style is appropriate.

EXERCISE

Jesus, of course, was the leader of the disciples. Read the following bits of the Bible and for each one plot Jesus' leadership on a continuum line, like the example below. Take just a little time to do this, it's not a full Bible study, just something to give you a feel for how Jesus varied his styles.

Autocrat——*——————————Non-leader

Mark 11:15–19 (the cleansing of the temple)

Bible bits to be plotted:

◆ **Mark 4:35–41 (Jesus calms the storm)**

◆ **John 3:1–13 (Jesus and Nicodemus)**

◆ **Luke 6:12–16 (Jesus chooses the Twelve)**

FEEDBACK

The important part of this exercise is not whereabouts you put Jesus on the line, but that Jesus' style changed to suit the need. The point is that Jesus adapted his style and we must learn from that example. People have told me that Jesus led in a certain way. I do not believe them; Jesus led in a variety of ways to suit the people, the culture of the day and his purposes at the time. That is the hallmark of an excellent leader.

EXERCISE

This is the final exercise about leadership styles. Think back to that group of young people that I first asked you to identify at the start of the chapter. In your notebook write a profile of the young person that acts as the leader most often in that group. Consider what type of leadership style they have and put forward some theories as to why they use that way of leading. You need to write a couple of paragraphs.

As a last piece of imagining, close your eyes and think about your role in that young people's group. Imagine them all there in their normal setting and then you walk in. What happens next? Do you become their leader? If so, why? Do you displace the person who normally leads? How do they feel about this? Do you just fit in with the group, blend into it? If so how do you achieve this?

Write up an account of this exercise in your book, it will probably take you about forty-five minutes.

FEEDBACK

These exercises ask you to think in terms of leadership styles and young people. I think now may be the time to point out to you something that is probably already obvious, and that is that young people don't read this kind of book! In other words they don't always conform to the patterns that people like myself write about. The young person who leads one group as an autocrat, may have nothing that you can see in their background or home life that would indicate that they have a need for power. That just goes to show that all theories need to be taken with a pinch of salt. All the same I think it is true that most young people who lead groups do so in a more authoritarian way than would an adult leading the same group. Would you agree? My theory on this is that young people have fewer situations in which they are the boss than most adults, so that when that opportunity does arise they exploit it. Young people's groups also have a tendency to be more fluid than adult groups. This means that leaders come and go fairly fast. The group is developing and changing so quickly that new leaders can emerge, and rule, and wane within months!

What I think is potentially the most interesting aspect of working with a group of young people is the effect we have on the group. What did you feel about this? Are you very much a leader? Do you naturally make the decisions within that group, influence the action or inaction of the group? If so, what does this say about Christians, or about Jesus? It's important to remember that the young people you work with will ultimately see you as what all Christians are like and, more worryingly, to see you as what Jesus is like. Acting in an overtly leader-like way will communicate to that group that Christians are about bossing you about, that they will take over your life and make all your choices. It may also be saying that this is what Jesus is like—an autocrat, with a big stick to chase you. To my mind, the Jesus that most young people would like to meet isn't like that.

This is all very well, but as I've indicated, just by being adults we take on leadership potential when we enter a group of young people. One of the questions I asked in the exercise was how do you achieve a blending in with the group? We cannot stop being adults, that is a fact—more importantly the young people wouldn't want us to, they value us as friends who are adults. We need our integrity. Pretending to be young people when we're not makes us ridiculous and, worse, makes us liars. I would say that the key to our role within groups of young people can be found in Philippians 2:5–11. This passage talks about Jesus (who could not stop being God in the same way that we cannot stop being adults) giving up the privileges of 'Godhood' to take on the likeness of a man, with all its inherent problems. I feel this is a pattern for us. We remain adults, as Jesus remained God, but we put aside its privileges and take on some of the difficulties that occur when you are a teenager.

Let me give you an example. Last week I was in school with a group of year 10 young people, I went to dinner with them. Year 10 pupils have to go in a certain door and wait in a certain queue. As an adult I am entitled to go in a more convenient door and go to the head of the queue. To be with that group, not as a leader but as a member, I chose to wait with them, and more than that, I chose not to mention that I could jump the queue, and to say when challenged by a sixth-former, 'No, I'm with Year 10 and we're not allowed in yet.' Do you see? The point is not that we lay down our adult role, but that we use it wisely; not that we never lead, but that we lead wisely, and in the knowledge of the wider implications of our leadership.

7 GROWING UP: THE OUTSIDE WORLD

Sam Adams

▌ COPING WITH BEREAVEMENT

In the first two sections of this chapter we will look at two major outside events that can have a deep and sometimes devastating effect on a teenager growing up: bereavement and divorce. Then we shall move on to look at what are often considered to be 'teenage problems' such as alcohol and drugs, eating disorders, sexual relationships, violence, crime and so on.

EXERCISE

This is a warm-up to get you thinking about bereavement, and to help you compare what you already know with the 'theory'.

In your notebook, write down every response to the death of someone close that you can think of. You can use personal experience, what you have observed in people around you and the way that grief is portrayed in novels, magazines, on the TV and so on. Soap operas are usually a good source of material!

This is a 'brainstorm' exercise—so spend ten minutes or so getting every example you can down on paper. Include feelings and actions.

Once you have done that, read through the 'input' below. After each

section, look back at your list, and mark every example that fits into the element or stage of grief being described by putting the relevant letter beside it. For example:

[B] unable to concentrate

[B/E] mother over-protective of other children after losing one

[C] crying

[E] feel picked on—'it's not fair'

INPUT

At any stage in life, coping with the death of someone close to us is difficult and disturbing. Death is the supreme example of the way in which the outside world can suddenly break into and upset our internal and personal world. Yet at the same time, it is a normal part of life, a daily happening, a vital element of our humanity.

Western culture does not help us to face and expect death. It is something of a taboo subject. At the root of this is an unwillingness to live with our own mortality. Death is seen as a thief, an enemy, a failure on the part of the medical profession. It is felt to be a disgrace, and encouraged to happen behind hospital screens and closed doors, where no one else need be confronted with it.

Nevertheless, much work has been done by counsellors and psychologists on the effects of bereavement. They have identified many common elements in grief:

A Numbness or denial. The immediate reaction of many people when a loved one dies is stunned disbelief. The feeling that 'this can't really be happening' often also brings a sense of personal unreality, an inability to feel anything. They are frozen, their feelings blunted, paralysed.

I didn't believe it though I knew it was true. I kept thinking it wasn't really happening and I was about to wake up. Everything else in the world stopped for a day or two. It seemed not to be actually happening. I remember lots of people coming round with flowers and stuff, but everything seemed totally unreal. When you're dreaming things seem fairly real at the time, but this was totally unreal. It was like there was me and there was everything else, and there was no connection.

'John', a teenager whose father died

This is a result of a shock that is too big to take in. By denying that it has happened, we unconsciously defend ourselves from the overwhelming impact of the loss.

For most people this stage doesn't last long, a few hours or a few days, and it is often brought to an end by a particular event such as seeing the body or attending the funeral, which helps to bring reality into focus.

B Alarm or fear.

No one ever told me that grief felt so much like fear. I am not afraid, but the sensation is like being afraid. The same fluttering in the stomach, the same restlessness, the yawning. I keep on swallowing.

C.S. Lewis

The loss of a loved one often leads to the physical reaction of fear. The body prepares to defend us from the perceived threat by getting ready for 'fight or flight'. The threat is psychological, but the reaction physical. People feel restless, edgy and panicky, especially when left alone. They may suffer from headaches, dizzy spells or sleeplessness.

C Searching.

I remember desperately wanting him to come up and give me a big hug, I wanted him to comfort me—why wasn't he there? It was confusing, because at the same time I knew the reason I wanted to be comforted was because he was gone.

'John'

The bereaved person is very likely to feel sudden waves of acute emotional distress, where they desperately pine or yearn for the lost one. These are real 'pangs of grief', periods of sighing, sobbing, crying out. People often find themselves unconsciously searching for the dead person, going to places they used to be together, scanning crowds for the familiar face. The goal is the missing person, but that goal is unattainable.

So many roads led thought to H.
I set out on one of them. But now
there's an impassable frontier post
across it. So many roads once; now
so many culs-de-sac.

C.S. Lewis

D Mitigation. These are the various conscious and more often unconscious ways of making the death hurt less. For example:

◆ talking to the dead person. 'Claire', a teenage girl who lost her mum, often sits with a photograph of her and talks to her. 'Kelly' writes letters to her dead grandfather.

◆ visiting the grave—to maintain a sense of relationship.

◆ delaying sorting out the dead person's things. 'Anna' used to get in her father's wardrobe because his clothes still smelt of him, and she wouldn't let her mum clean them and give them away.

◆ keeping some things the same as a kind of memorial, perhaps a room, or an everyday activity because that's how the dead person would have done it or liked it and so on.

◆ may have vivid dreams about the person as though they were still alive.

◆ may hide personal effects and avoid sorting things out because they can't yet face it.

All of these are constructive if they are helping the person to deal with the loss at a pace which they can cope with.

E Anger and guilt. This is an aspect of grief which can shock both the bereaved person and the people caring for them. Anger may be directed against the person who died—why did you leave me; why did you do this to me? Anger may be against life itself, against the medical staff or anyone who may have been responsible in any way for the death; against God.

I felt incredibly cheated. I thought it wasn't fair that she'd seen my sister grow up and get married, but I was only sixteen and I wanted her to see me do all that. She never even met Kevin [her boyfriend]. I felt very angry about that, and with her . . . for a while I blamed whatever God might be up there.

'Claire'

This anger is often experienced as a general irritability and bitterness towards everyone and everything. Friends and would-be helpers can find this behaviour extremely difficult, and may end up on the receiving end of some of this anger from the bereaved!

The flip side of anger is guilt, that is anger directed against oneself. Most bereaved people experience at least some guilt. This may be for a number of reasons:

◆ they feel guilty for things said or never said, now that it is too late

◆ they feel guilty about arguments left unresolved

◆ they feel guilty that they didn't do enough to prevent the death

◆ they feel guilty for having consciously or unconsciously having wished the person dead, and now feel irrationally responsible for the death.

F Gaining a new identity. If we live in a close relationship with another person, that relationship is a part of our identity. The relationship is an important landmark in our internal map of who we are. Part of who I am is my father's/my mother's daughter. We rely on significant people in our lives for their reactions, responses and opinions to tell us what we are like and who we are.

So the loss of someone close will profoundly affect our sense of identity. For example the death of a spouse means someone is no longer married, perhaps becomes a single parent. A major task of the grieving process is giving up the old identity, in which this relationship was a foundation, and to form and accept a new identity, in which this person and the relationship with them is no longer actively present (although memories of them may still play a part).

These various elements, from initial numbness to gaining a new identity, are all normal and healthy parts of the grieving process. They may not happen in the order given above, but they are usually all present. Grief is a long-term process. The death of a parent or spouse is considered to have the most profound impact on someone's life, and it usually takes between three and five years to achieve a new identity, a new sense of who one is and one's life in which the dead person is not an integral part.

Grieving becomes unhealthy when the bereaved person gets 'stuck' in one or more of these responses, and is unable or unwilling to move on towards recovery and the process of rebuilding their life.

FEEDBACK

How did you get on with classifying your answers? You may have found that some of the examples you gave fitted into more than one category. Do you have any left over, that didn't fit into any of the elements or stages of grief suggested above? If so, are you able to group them together in any way, as a different category or categories?

Having compared your knowledge of bereavement with the theory, what do you think of the theory? Is it a set of ideas that you find helpful, and could use in your youthwork?

We are now going to move on from looking at bereavement in general, to focusing on the particular impact it has on teenagers, and how we can be of help as youthworkers.

EXERCISE

Think back to chapter 3. Can you remember the main 'tasks' of adolescence? What is this stage all about in terms of psychological development? In what ways does the experience of bereavement challenge this, and make the task of growing up more difficult:

◆ **when a teenager loses anyone they are close to?**

◆ **when a teenager loses a parent?**

Spend about fifteen minutes on each question, and try to think of at least three points for each of them. Here's an example:

Falling in love—this is a normal part of being a teenager, and helps them to move on from the family. However, if someone they love (friend, family or boyfriend/girlfriend) dies, this may make them unwilling to risk falling in love because they have experienced such pain in losing someone like this.

Now find your own links between being a teenager and bereavement.

EEDBACK

I hope you have had a go at this exercise before reading my answers—it is an important skill to develop. Being able to think through how a particular problem will impact the growing up process will help you in your youthwork. It will help you to understand why a young person is reacting the way they are to a crisis in their life. And in my experience such understanding gives us the patience and tolerance we so often need really to be able to get alongside and be of help.

Don't worry—you'll be getting more practice at this later in the chapter!

Back to the subject in hand—bereavement and teenagers.

A TEENAGER LOSING ANYONE THEY ARE CLOSE TO

1   Adolescence is a time when people often feel insecure as they are leaving their old source of security (the family) and trying to build a new one (based on themselves, their friends, partners and so on). Someone close dying will make them feel even more insecure. They may also feel very vulnerable, as though anyone else they care

about might die, or that they themselves might die.

2   Peer relationships—it is important to adolescents to feel that they are normal, that they fit in. Losing someone close to them will make them feel different, that they stand out. Their friends may not know how to respond to their grief, so they may feel very isolated. All these factors may well result in them not telling their friends, or hiding their feelings—which will not help them to grieve.

3   Being a teenager is about beginning to find and experience personal power, to flex psychological muscles such as willpower, to be able to change things. The death of someone close will give a teenager the opposite experience—powerlessness, inability to change anything. Grief is often accompanied by a great apathy. At a time when most young people are starting to go out into the world with the expectation of making some impact upon it, the grieving adolescent may just withdraw.

4   Identity—the major task of adolescence is to form a firm identity on which to build the rest of one's life. An important element of our identity will be the close relationships in our life. When someone close to us dies, this shakes our sense of who we are, and for a teenager who is still in the process of putting their identity together, this can threaten to upset the whole deal.

A TEENAGER LOSING A PARENT

1   Independence—at a time when teenagers are moving away from the family and becoming more and more invested in relationships with peers, the death of a

parent can affect this in either direction. It may undermine their emerging sense of autonomy so that they feel unable to become independent at that point. Or it may lead to an exaggerated sense of self-sufficiency, as they try to feel more independent then they are.

2   Separation—teenagers need something solid to separate from, something firm to bounce themselves against in order to feel separate and different. It is usually the parents who provide this. However much a teenager resents being nagged about their homework, having to be in by a set time and so on, they need this structure in place if they are going to make a break from it. When a parent dies, this structure is shaken, and may collapse if the other parent is not coping well with their grief.

3   Adolescent rebellion—this serves to put some distance between teenagers who are struggling for independence and their parents. If a parent dies whilst this sort of power struggle is going on, the teenager may feel very guilty. They may have consciously wished that parent dead. They may never have said sorry for hurtful things they have said or done. They may somehow feel responsible. This will exaggerate the normal feeling of guilt often associated with grief.

4   Responsibility—the death of a parent may well leave the adolescent in the position of having to take on much more responsibility within the family. This will contrast with their peers who will be enjoying the normal carelessness of youth.

This is by no means an exhaustive list. I hope you were able to find some other links. Most of these answers show that the combination of adolescence and bereavement is likely to make both growing up and grieving more difficult. This may mean that a young person gets stuck in one of the phases of grief we looked at earlier; or that they get stuck in a phase of growing up. This is where it can be very important to have a caring adult around who is not caught up in the situation, but able to offer support. Let's now look at how, as Christian youthworkers, we can help a teenager who is grieving.

INPUT

How we can help:

A We need to come to terms with our own anxieties about death. We will not be able to help others if we don't face this or our own sense of unresolved grief.

B We need to know what we believe about death and life after death. How will you answer a young person who wants to know if their mum has gone to heaven?

C We need to be able to simply sit with them and listen, to be able to put our own sense of helplessness to one side and be able to 'hold' their grief. Teenagers may be able to express their feelings more openly than adults, to just cry and cry. We need to be able to stay with them, to allow them to do this.

D We need to give them permission not to grieve. They are teenagers, and need to let their hair down and have fun, to distract themselves from their grief for a while. But they may feel guilty for this, and we can help them to see that this doesn't mean that they loved the deceased person any less.

E We need to be able to reassure the teenager that what they are experiencing is normal (knowing some theory is helpful here!). People often feel they are losing their minds as they experience the intense and contradictory feelings of grief.

F We also need to stress that everyone will grieve differently, to reassure them that, for example, if they cry less than a sibling that doesn't mean they love less.

G We need to respect their need for solitude. Teenagers need privacy, and in times of major stress they find it particularly helpful to have some space and time alone.

H We need to encourage teenagers to express all their feelings. Teenagers, even more so than most other people, will particularly shy away from these painful feelings. They will try to escape or avoid the feelings that they don't understand. Our support and empathy, making it OK to feel like this, can be very important.

I We need to be sensitive to the different reactions to bereavement of the two genders. Boys often behave more aggressively, often challenging authority. They are more likely to increase their use of drugs and alcohol as a way of punishing themselves and others. Girls, on the other hand, often express a longing for comfort and reassurance, and want to be held and consoled. This may lead to an increase in sexual activity. These contrasting responses show the effect of social conditioning. If you are male, it is acceptable to be angry, if you are female it is acceptable to be upset, but not the other way around.

J We need to be sensitive to the increased guilt that may be felt by teenagers, because of the power struggle they may have been engaged in with their deceased parent. It is common in adolescence to be very critical of one's parents, as we move from a childhood idealization of them, to a more realistic view. Again, being able to explain that this is normal may be of great help.

K We need to be there first and foremost for the young person. It is very important that they have support outside of the family. 'Claire' says of her friends, 'They kept me happy, I felt I could talk to them. To my friends I was the only person who loved my mum; I wanted to feel I loved her more than anyone else did. I didn't want to talk to others who loved her just as much.' Having someone to talk to can prevent withdrawal and isolation.

L We need to be prepared to tolerate anger and hostility from the young person. It is important not to take this personally! It may be a way (particularly for boys) of trying to draw attention to the distress that they feel, as well as being a normal element of grief.

M We need to be patient, to be prepared to hear the same things over and over, to keep talking about the dead person rather than to avoid the subject. Grieving takes a long time.

EXERCISE

Re-read points A–M of how we can help, and pick out the two or three of those things that you would find most difficult to do.

In your notebook, answer the following questions for each of the things you have selected:

1   Why do you think you would find this difficult?

2 Can you pin-point the core problem for you in this area?

3 Do you have any experience of having found this difficult in the past (not necessarily in dealing with someone who is bereaved)? If so, can you summarize your experience?

4 How could you improve your skill/ability in this area?

5 Set yourself a couple of achievable learning goals in this area, for example, concerning point B:

◆ Look up the subject in the Bible.

◆ Ask two people whose views I respect what they think on the subject.

◆ Get someone to role-play being a non-Christian teenager, so that I can practice being able to explain what I believe to them.

6 Decide how you are going to evaluate your progress in this area.

EEDBACK

This exercise is a form of 'self-supervision'—a way of thinking critically about our own practice, and looking to build on our strengths and weaknesses. I hope you are able to have a go at your learning goals.

It is well worth coming back to this in a couple of weeks, and seeing if you think you would be more able to deal with these aspects of helping a bereaved teenager.

If you would like a little more practice on paper, here is a longer quotation from a teenager:

Now, nearly a year later, my grief is uncontrollable. I don't know what to do. I can't handle it. I feel so empty, so lost, and I can't believe that she is actually dead. She was a really good person. She was always there for me, she was funny, pretty, popular, intelligent and talented. It seems so unfair that she died. Why her? Why not me or someone else?

I miss her desperately. Many people have told me that the pain gets better but that doesn't help me to accept that she's gone.

It was the worst experience of my life. One of the sad things is that no one talks about her any more and no one mentions death when they're around me, the subject is always carefully avoided. They can't see that I want to talk about it, that I need to talk about it.

'Kerry', whose best friend died aged 14

If you were to meet 'Kerry' now, if she was to start coming along to the youth club that you help at, or wherever it is that you meet and get to know young people, how would you go about offering her help?

I'll leave you to work out your own response to her needs.

▦ DIVORCE

INTRODUCTION

In this section, we will be looking at the impact of divorce and family break-up on teenagers. Our main material for this will be quotations from teenagers who have lived through this experience.

The aims of this section are:

◆ to gain a better understanding of the effect divorce has on the lives of teenagers

◆ to develop skills in thinking through how outside problems like this can affect the growing-up process

◆ to begin to think about how the 'good news' might relate to teenagers experiencing such problems.

I hope that doesn't sound too gruelling! If you can get to grips with these things in this section, you will be able to get much more out of the last two sections, where I intend to make you do much more of the work.

Anyway, on with the subject at hand.

INPUT

Family break-up is an increasingly common occurrence in our society. One in three marriages ends in divorce. The Family Policy Studies Centre estimates that one in five children now alive in the UK will see their parents divorce before they reach the age of sixteen. These figures, of course, only refer to families where the parents were married. It is even harder to measure the increase in family break-up where there is no legal process, just separation.

On the whole, separation and divorce is something in which the children are mere bystanders. It is about failure in the relationship between their parents, and they have little or no say in the whole affair. Yet it is an event which will profoundly affect their lives.

Below are the common, central themes in a child's experience of their parents' divorce, regardless of age:

Divorce is frightening. They have a heightened sense of their own vulnerability. They become consciously preoccupied with concern that their needs, both present and future, will go unattended. These fears reflect their confusion about their future relationship with their parents. They are intensely afraid of being abandoned by a parent.

Divorce is a time of sadness and yearning. An enormous sense of loss: the loss of the family as an ongoing presence, loss of sense of continuity and structure. They experience emptiness, tearfulness, difficulty in concentrating, chronic fatigue and troublesome dreams. It is very common to have fantasies of reconciliation.

Divorce is a time of worry. They are concerned for their parents' emotional stability and capacity to manage without the other's help. They worry about parental suicidal impulses, possible accidents, chronic illness—the possible loss of their second parent for whatever reason. They worry about the changed economic and social realities, new partners, remarriage and so on.

Divorce is a time of feeling rejected. The departure of one parent is experienced as demonstrating a diminished interest in them, the child. They will have nagging questions about their own loveability.

Divorce is a lonely time. The child is likely to spend much more time alone.

Divorce is a time of conflicting loyalties. They feel pulled by love and loyalty in both directions. Most parents openly compete for their children's love and allegiance. A step in the direction of one parent is experienced as a betrayal of the other.

Divorce is a time of anger. There is often a rise in aggression. The child sees the divorce as an act of selfishness by the parents, giving primary consideration to their own needs and only secondary consideration to the children. They bitterly resent the destruction of their family and home, and feel betrayed by the unbecoming, immoral behaviour of their parents.

Can you see any common links with the experience of the death of a parent (see the previous section)? In bereavement, however, the child has the opportunity to resolve their feelings by working through their grief and coming to terms with the fact that the parent is no longer there. In family break-up this is much more difficult, as the parent is still alive but choosing not to be in a close, parental relationship, and this is often experienced as ongoing rejection by the child. This is much harder to resolve and come to terms with, as there is always the possibility that the absent parent may walk back into their life in some way.

EXERCISE

This is a long exercise, so please take your time over it. Below are eight subsections, with quotations from teenagers who have experienced parental divorce talking about different aspects of that experience. From each subsection pick the quotation that strikes you most— you should end up with eight quotations! Then use these quotations to work on for the rest of this exercise.

1 Changes in living arrangements

'Cooking and washing dishes are not a man's job.'

'My mum had more money problems when my dad was here.'

'I'm fifteen and I'm given so much freedom— sometimes it's a pain because you want someone to be really strict with you.'

'Having gone from a really tight family to having nothing—I've had to bring myself up.'

'We're a lot more independent now as individuals, especially my mum. The house is run by all of us now.'

'I know my mum has to work to pay the bills and all that, but sometimes I'd rather just see her than eat. I'd rather be cold and hungry than lonely.'

2 Reasons for the divorce—the explanations given to the children

'My mum—she told me everything. She couldn't explain a lot when I was five, but when I was older she could tell me as much as I was able to understand. She wouldn't hide anything.'

'For about a year I didn't realize we wouldn't be returning home.'

'I didn't want to know what was going on; I thought it was just a passing phase.'

'I asked once or twice but mum just got annoyed with me so I gave up asking. I still don't know why they split up.'

'It really pissed me off I was never actually talked to and asked what I thought.'

'I kept asking questions because I found it difficult to believe that my parents had split. I always got the same answer, that my father had hit my mother. If he hadn't hit her that night he'd probably still be here.'

'They both said "you're not having them" so they said we could go into a home—that really upset me.'

'At one time my parents were in love, then they weren't. Did it have something to do with me? Perhaps if I had been a better daughter, a prettier daughter, it would have made me more valuable, more worth staying for.'

3 Support from friends, family and school

'You don't really talk about things like that.'

'I tried to hide from my friends that my mother had left, because I didn't like the idea of having no mother—I was embarrassed.'

'I didn't like telling anybody; I tried to keep it a secret.'

'At school, I just sat there and couldn't think about anything except my parents and family. After a while the teachers stopped getting on at me, I suppose someone must have told them.'

'I tried, not to forget, but to forget at school.'

'You're the first person who's ever bothered to ask me how I felt.'

4 Their personal response to the divorce

'I felt sick and couldn't get it out of my mind that my father had left; I took a couple of years to get used to it.'

'I was very upset and my mother knew, but she did nothing to get my father to return.'

'I was worried about not having my mother in the house and longed for her to return. Depression set in quite a few times and I'd sneak away to my room and play records and not speak to anyone.'

'I couldn't understand it or get to grips with it. After a couple of weeks I started going through a bad patch, losing my temper, fighting with my brother.'

'I wasn't surprised or anything. I was just a bit gutted.'

'I felt that the rug had been pulled out from under me. I cried and I begged and begged. I tried to talk sense to my mum till I was almost mute.'

'The beliefs which gave me the ability to deal effectively with life were blown apart for me by my dad's behaviour. I felt like I was taking a leaking boat, namely me, into the storm.'

5 Their feelings towards their parents

'I was very angry, really angry, I'm still angry. He was the one that always had the money, while my mum went short. I really hate him now.'

'I'm always wondering why my mum left me.'

'My dad was sad all the time and my mum was angry all the time and we felt annoyed with her.'

'I'm a proper little daddy's girl, would snuggle up with him in front of the TV for a couple of hours, and it was really hard when I couldn't any more.'

'I feel more responsible for my mum— I'm all she's got. I felt guilty of neglecting her as she hasn't got a husband.'

'You felt you were doing something for them if your crying made them stop arguing.'

'Christmas is a hard one—you've got two families and you don't want to hurt either of them.'

'I've always had a dream that they'll come together again.'

6 Access to the non-custodial parent

'It seemed natural to go out with him. It was coming home that was difficult.'

'My mum never said anything about visiting my dad; I would have wanted to see him.'

'My dad is just a man I know.'

'I never knew when I would see my father next—I could never be sure there ever would be a next time.'

'When my mum drives me to my dad's for the weekend she won't even go up to the house let alone inside. She just shoves me out of the car and roars off. I feel like a real creep for wanting to see my dad, but I won't stop going to see him.'

'He gave us sweets, trying to keep you happy, trying to buy us.'

'He treated me like the little girl I'd been four years earlier.'

'He always asked if she had a boyfriend. He's not exactly rotten, but he would like a chance to stop paying her money.'

7 Parent's new partners

'One thing I could never get used to were dad's girlfriends! Spending most weekends with him, I got to see quite a few of them. But just as I really got to like one, things would change and then I'd have to go through the embarrassment of meeting another one.'

'He suddenly appeared. I couldn't stand him. I hated him. If he wasn't that happy about kids, he shouldn't have come to live with us.'

'It felt good living with him. Mum could have coped on her own, but having a father made life an awful lot easier.'

'I went through a stage, if she brought a man home I thought it was really horrible, but now she's completely different if there's someone about. She's a bit off if she's just broken off with someone.'

'I was a real devil to my step-father. I felt he was always picking on me and I was jealous of no longer being mum's best helper. My younger brothers liked our step-father and they got on so well with him I felt even more pushed out. I felt as though I was shut up in a dark cupboard all by myself while hearing the rest of my family playing and laughing in the garden.'

'Dad found more time for her that what he did for me. I'd rather wash dishes than have her here.'

'He's getting older and we'd like to see him married because we wouldn't like to leave him by himself when we leave home.'

8 Their own futures

'I won't marry young because I want to develop my interests and my skills first. Love and respect are necessary, but companionship is the most important thing in a marriage. The trouble with my parents was that they didn't respect each other at all. Their only common interest was us kids.'

'Even though mum and dad are dishonest and I used to be, I suddenly stopped lying. I don't know why, I just stopped lying last year. I decided that I didn't want to be like them and that I would tell the truth.'

'It keeps coming up—however hard you try to get away from it.'

'It's changed my whole values of life—completely changed them around. Before I would say no to smoking, now I smoke and don't see what's wrong with it. I can get away with it now.'

'I used to dream of marrying and having kids, but now I don't want to get married because I've seen how it ends. Mum and dad hate each other now.'

'I'd be ten times more careful now before I married or had children—I wouldn't want to put any children through divorce or separation.'

'I think the idea of living with someone before you get married is a good idea rather than marrying, having kids and finding it's all a disaster and put your kids through it all.'

'I think you should marry if you're going to have kids—children are a commitment like marriage.'

You should have picked a quotation from each section that particularly strikes you. Now write each one out at the top of a separate page in your workbook, so you will have space to work through the following questions for each quotation—this should give you lots of practice!

◆ **What feelings is the young person expressing?**

◆ **What feelings does this quotation arouse in you?**

◆ **How does this young person's experience relate to the theory on pages 124–125?**

◆ **What does this example tell you about how the experience of parental divorce affects the growing-up process in adolescence? Think back to chapter 3 and the ways we made links in the last section between the tasks of adolescence and the effect bereavement has on teenagers.**

◆ **How might the good news begin to interact with this young person's situation?**

Pick just four of your eight quotations for this part of the exercise.

Try to be really creative here. The good news is *not* that Jesus died for our sins. What I mean is, the good news is not *only* that Jesus died for our sins. To someone who knows nothing about God, the good news is a much bigger thing, encompassing the whole of life. The salvation that we are offered through Christ is the way into all the many promises and gifts that God has for us.

The first ever 'mission', evangelistic talk and altar-call all rolled into one is recorded in Acts chapter 3. Peter's call to faith is:

Repent, then, and turn to God, so that your sins may be wiped out, that times of refreshing may come from the Lord, and that he may send . . . Jesus.

Acts 3:19–20 (NIV)

The good news is not repentance, but the times of refreshing and the presence of Jesus which will result from repenting and turning to God. Or to put it another way, God so loved the world that he sent his only Son *so that* whoever believes in him should not perish but have eternal life.

Have a go—start by thinking of the feelings and needs this young person is expressing, and then try to find a way in which God promises to meet those needs, or in which 'who God is' provides an answer to their situation.

FEEDBACK

WHAT FEELINGS IS THE YOUNG PERSON EXPRESSING?

Here is a list of common feelings:

sorrow	depression
anger	insecurity
resentment	longing
jealousy	annoyance
confusion	responsible
resignation	frustration
bitterness	ignored
isolation	used/abused
rejection	cynical
victimized	abandoned
disbelief	concerned
embarrassment	vulnerable
shame	betrayed
anxiety	bereaved.

This is by no means an exhaustive list. Did you find any of these feelings? Have you written the same feelings for more than one quotation? Are there feelings that you think are more common than others among young people who experience parental divorce?

WHAT FEELINGS DOES THIS QUOTATION AROUSE IN YOU?

I hope you were able to be honest here.

◆ Were any of your feelings the same as those you had attributed to the young person?

◆ Where do you think your feelings are coming from?

◆ Do they relate to things you have experienced in the past?

◆ How far are they a direct response to what the young person has said?

◆ Are your responses in part because you have a sense of what 'normal' or 'ideal' family life should be like, and you are comparing this young person's situation to that?

It is important to have an idea of where our responses are coming from, so we can evaluate if they are appropriate and helpful for our youthwork.

HOW DOES THIS YOUNG PERSON'S EXPERIENCE RELATE TO THE THEORY ON PAGES 124–125?

Did you find that the quotations backed up or contradicted the theory?

WHAT DOES THIS EXAMPLE TELL YOU ABOUT HOW THE EXPERIENCE OF PARENTAL DIVORCE AFFECTS THE GROWING-UP PROCESS IN ADOLESCENCE?

If I worked through all the examples, we'd be here into next week, so I'll just summarize the main effects divorce has on teenagers, and leave you to assess whether the quotations show that this is borne out in experience.

A Teenagers experience their divorcing parents as leaving them—at a time when they would normally be working towards leaving their parents. It is as though the parents have taken the centre stage within the family at a time the teenagers should have it. The adults are felt to be changing more rapidly than their youngsters; it is the grown-ups changing the roles within the family, rather than the teenagers.

B Adolescents often feel that the time available to them for growing up has been foreshortened by the divorce. They feel hurried and pressed to achieve independence quickly. They feel robbed of time just to play and relax. Divorce can either drive things forward at a much faster rate, or bring everything to a grinding halt.

C Divorce often severely weakens normal family functions such as providing discipline, external structure and controls. This can leave adolescents feeling vulnerable to their own newly strengthened sexual and aggressive impulses. They are left surrounded by all the temptations of the teenage world, without the supports that would hold them in a straight course.

D At a time when teenagers are coming to terms with their own new identity as sexual people, the perception of their parents as sexual people (as they find new partners and so on) can be startling and unsettling. The fact that many divorcees date people much younger than themselves can add to the teenager's distress—their parent's new lover may be nearer to their own age than their parent's.

E The changes associated with divorce often mean that the parents' preoccupations and behaviour is parallel to their adolescent children, and threatens to narrow the generation gap. Parents are asking, 'Who am I? Where am I going?' Most distressing for the teenager is the conscious or unconscious feeling of competition from their parents. This is painful because they feel betrayed and deserted by parents they had fully expected to support their own growth towards adulthood.

F Parents tend to be very distressed by the divorce, and this is disturbing for their children. Teenagers feel the need for strong and stable adults who could provide a steady, reliable and supportive presence during the many crises of growing up. Instead they feel that the tables have been turned and that they are needed to take responsibility for the needy parent, whilst being fearful of being caught in the net of parental unhappiness.

G The normal teenage preoccupations of sex, marriage, love and search for a partner are now coloured with the fear that their parents' divorce foreshadows their own future failure in these areas.

H The teenager's attempts to understand what led to the divorce and to sort out their parents' different roles in it often speeds up emotional and intellectual maturity and growth. Adolescents soberly consider their parents' experiences and draw thoughtful conclusions for their own future.

I Research has shown that:

◆ Many teenagers recognize their parents' unhappiness and need for help, and take on protective and helpful roles, sharing household responsibility and care of younger children with competence, sensitivity and pride.

◆ Many teenagers respond by attempting to increase their distance from the family crisis and their parents. They enter a variety of activities which keep them away from home.

◆ Of all the age groups of children experiencing parental divorce, teenagers show the most damaging effects. It has been estimated that two-thirds engage in some type of illegal or self-destructive behaviour, or both, following the divorce. Boys tend towards serious traffic offences, drug sales and theft; girls tend towards drug and alcohol abuse. In both genders, sexual activity is increased, especially in families where the amount of parental control has decreased.

◆ Over a year after the divorce, a third of teenagers show signs of even greater distress.

◆ Ten years later, memories of the trauma of divorce are still overwhelmingly vivid and they are outspoken in their views that marriage is not to be entered into lightly or impulsively and that they want to avoid divorce for *their* own children's sake.

HOW MIGHT THE GOOD NEWS BEGIN TO INTERACT WITH THIS YOUNG PERSON'S SITUATION?

I will give you eight examples of how I would start to think about God and what might be good news. Obviously, a short quotation means that we have to assume an awful lot about the young person and their situation. But it also simplifies the task for us—we are only trying to respond to this one comment by them, not their whole life.

Please read my suggestions, and then re-read your own answers. Don't worry if I have said something completely different to you—the point of the exercise is for you to develop your skill in this area, not for you to become a clone of Sam Adams, or skilled in reading my mind!

1 'I'm fifteen and I'm given so much freedom—sometimes it's a pain because you want someone to be really strict with you.'

Part of the good news to this young person might be that God cares enough about them to have rules/laws/guidelines that he wants them to keep for their own welfare.

2 'At one time my parents were in love, then they weren't. Did it have something to do with me? Perhaps if I had been a better daughter, a prettier daughter, it would have made me more valuable, more worth staying for.'

Part of the good news to this young person might be that to God the Father they are a very valuable and precious daughter, worth staying for (and worth sending Jesus for). Also, God promises never to leave us alone as orphans.

3 'I didn't like telling anybody; I tried to keep it a secret.'

Part of the good news to this young person might be that God already knows their 'secret', they don't have to tell him. Also, that this 'secret' won't make any difference to how God feels about them, or how God will respond to them.

4 'I wasn't surprised or anything, I was just a bit gutted about it.'

Part of the good news to this young person might be that God is also not surprised, but gutted that this has happened. God is hurting for everyone in this situation, and God is angry that people are hurting each other in this way.

5 'Christmas is a hard one—you've got two families and you don't want to hurt either of them.'

Part of the good news to this young person might be that God understands about being torn between two things (for example, Jesus in the garden of Gethsemane), and can help to find solutions to this. God also promises to help us withstand outside pressures.

6 'My mum never said anything about visiting my dad; I would have wanted to see him.'

Part of the good news to this young person might be that God thinks this is unfair, that they have been robbed of something

important. God values family relationships a great deal, but says that having a relationship with him is even more important.

7 'He suddenly appeared, I couldn't stand him. I hated him. If he wasn't that happy about kids, he should never have come to live with us.'

Part of the good news to this young person might be that God won't act like this in their life. He won't impose himself uninvited. Also, that unlike this man, God wants them to share their everyday life with him.

8 'I used to dream of marrying and having kids, but now I don't want to get married because I've seen how it ends. Mum and Dad hate each other now.'

Part of the good news to this young person might be that God wants them to have dreams and ideals. Also, that things don't have to turn out for them the same way that they have for their parents. Christ offers them a new start, free from the effects of the past, and his help to make dreams into reality.

This part of the exercise is by far the hardest, so don't worry if you struggled. I found it very difficult with some of the quotations, and I'm not sure that all my suggestions hold water. Fortunately, this is just an exercise, but it should help us to think through what Christ offers the young people that we work with.

■ TEENAGE PROBLEMS: AN OVERVIEW

INTRODUCTION

In this section we are going to look at the whole phenomena of 'teenage problems', before going on to examine one such issue in depth in the next section.

Before you start on this section, make sure you have at least one magazine marketed for teenagers in front of you—you will need one with a 'problem page', so most of the music ones are no good. Check out with the young people that you work with what they read, so you are buying something they spend their money on. You never know, you might even learn something!

Make a list of everything you can think of that is considered to be a teenage problem in society. This is a brainstorm, so take no more than about ten minutes. I'll start you off with some of the most obvious:

◆ under-age sex

◆ vandalism

◆ drugs.

Look over your list. Having got all the ideas down on paper, let's now look at them more critically.

◆ How many of these 'problems' have ever been a part of your life?

◆ How many of these problems apply exclusively to teenagers?

◆ How many of the things in your list would be regarded by a teenager as a problem?

◆ How many of these things do you think are getting worse, and why?

◆ How many of these things do you think are improving, and why?

These questions should help you to think through who is defining what things are 'teenage problems'. It is important to realize how much we are influenced by the way things are portrayed in the media. For example car crime is commonly regarded as a teenage problem, and its increase seen as an indication of the decline in moral standards among young people. But another major factor in increasing car crime is the increase in the number of cars! And who is questioning the morality of owning a car when so many people in our world do not have the basic necessities of life?

It is also important to remember that for an individual young person, any one of these 'problems' may in fact be a symptom rather than a cause. In the first two sections of this chapter we looked at young people coping with death and family break-up. Many who struggle to cope with these events in their lives, turn to or are drawn towards some of these 'problems' to find release, excitement, expression or obliteration of their feelings.

At the same time, growing up is affected by the world in which it happens. More young people use drugs these days because more drugs are more readily available to young people. More young people have sex outside of marriage these days because society's views on sexual freedom have changed. Young people grow up within the culture of their society, whilst at the same time challenging that culture with their own 'sub-culture'.

EXERCISE

Let's look now at the things which young people consider to be problems as they grow up. You should have a secular magazine aimed at teenagers. These are mostly girls' mags, but they often have problems from boys too!

(I couldn't find a Christian magazine for teenagers with a problem page—does this mean that Christian teenagers don't have problems? I think not—you'll probably find that they are just as likely as anyone else to read the problem page in a normal mag. Watch a group of teenagers when someone buys the latest copy—they often go straight for the problem page, and read out all the 'juicy' stuff and then discuss both the problem and the answer given.)

Turn to the problem page, and read all the letters and answers given. Then answer the following questions:

1   Summarize each 'problem' into one word or a short headline, for example 'Abortion' or 'Low self-esteem'.

2   Compare these headlines with the list you made earlier of 'teenage problems':

◆ Are some of them the same? Can you classify these in any way?

◆ Are some of them different? Can you classify these in any way?

◆ What does this tell you about the things that teenagers experience as problems?

Now pick two of the problems that are as different from each other as possible and work on just these for the rest of the questions.

3   Read the problem letters very carefully. Why does this young person consider their situation to be a problem?

◆ What feelings are involved?

◆ What values/morals does this show them to have?

◆ What 'ideal' are they comparing their situation to?

◆ Where do you think these ideas have come from?

4   Read the answers given very carefully. How is the 'agony aunt/ uncle' responding?

◆ What feelings are involved?

◆ What values/morals does this show them to have?

◆ What 'ideal' are they comparing the young person's situation to?

◆ Where do you think these ideas have come from?

5   What do you think of the advice being given?

6   Now have a go at being an 'agony aunt/uncle' yourself, and write an answer to both of these problems—up to 200 words each. What advice would you want to give this young person, and why?

EEDBACK

Most people find other people's problems fascinating! Most of our media entertainment is built on that fact. We like to compare ourselves to other people, either because we associate ourselves and our situation with theirs, or so we can feel good about the difference between them and us— 'I'd never do anything so stupid!'

Most of the 'problems' which teenagers write to these mags about are to do with relationships—either having them or not having them. The results of these relationships problems may be some of the things generally thought of as 'teenage problems' such as suicide, abortion, eating disorders and so on. In this respect, teenagers are like the rest of society, for whom relationships are generally the key part of their lives—the things that give life meaning, and make it worth living (or not worth living).

We all operate within a worldview, made up of our values, attitudes, beliefs, ethical framework, experiences, hopes, expectations and ideals. It is this worldview that defines for us what we experience as 'problems'. For example, most Christians would consider sex outside of marriage to be a problem, because they believe that God considers this to be a sin, and because they see the consequences of such sex as harmful to people's wellbeing. However, many non-Christians consider sex outside of marriage to be no problem at all, and indeed may consider a lack of sexual activity to be a problem and bad for one's wellbeing!

Obviously we don't construct our worldview in a vacuum. We put it together as we grow up, absorbing many ideas from the world around us. Key sources for these ideas will be:

- parents and wider family
- school
- friends
- media
- the law of the land
- the local community
- traditions and customs
- religion and places of worship (church, mosque, temple, synagogue and so on)
- our personal experience.

One thing we need to be very aware of as Christian youthworkers is that the worldview of the young people with whom we work and our own worldview may be very different. When young people come to us with their problems we are faced with an ethical dilemma. Should we offer them help and advice within their worldview or within ours, or neither of those, but some third 'societal norm'?

Part of the answer to this question will be defined by the context within which we work and the expectations of our 'employers' (whether we are paid or not!) or the organization under whose auspices we work.

Part of the answer will be defined by why that young person has come to us—their expectations of us. They may have asked us precisely because they want to know what God thinks on the issue. They may have asked us because they think we will listen to their concerns and help them to find their own answers. They may have asked us because they think we are 'experts', and so they are expecting impartial advice.

Part of the answer will be defined by us as individuals—our worldview will help us to determine what we think is the right thing to do. Responding to young people when they are in need is a vital part of our work, a test of the relationships we have been building with them and often a time when faith and the meaning of life become real issues for teenagers. At the same time, we need to be sure that we are not taking advantage of their need. Brainwashing and indoctrination is much easier with people who are already unsure of themselves and dependent on others for help. With this warning in mind, let's have another go at responding to teenage problems.

EXERCISE

Now that we have looked at 'problems' from the young person's point of view and have seen some of the advice that they seek and get, let us move on to look at 'problems' from our perspective, as Christian youthworkers seeking to make Jesus known to the young people with whom we work.

Below are a selection of letters to problem pages from a variety of young people's magazines. This time you will not have the answer given by the professional 'agony aunts/uncles' to look at. Read them all through and pick two that particularly strike you.

A   I need a boyfriend

I'm so unhappy and ugly, and I have spots on my face. My friends say I'm not to put myself down, and that I'm pretty, but they're just saying that so they don't hurt my feelings. All the boys I fancy either don't like me or have girlfriends, and they probably think I'm ugly. Do you think it's because I'm going for the wrong boys, or because I'm ugly? I don't think I'll ever have a boyfriend.
Girl, age 15

B   Can't cope with girl-problems

I'm going out with a 16 year-old girl. Recently she keeps going on about her periods and PMT and tampons and things. And I don't know how to react as I am not very well-informed on girls' problems. What should I do? On top of this I think she's a lesbian as she never gets intimate with me, although I've been seeing her for a while. And she talks erotically about some of her friends. This worries me as I love her very much and don't want to lose her.
Boy

C   I can't stop thinking about him

Two months ago I split up with my boyfriend of six months and the problem is I still love him so much. As soon as we split up he started going out with a new girl, and every time I see them together I feel really sad and want to cry. I can't stop thinking about him. We still talk to each other quite frequently on the phone, and I think this is probably making things worse. I know I should forget him but I just can't. Nobody understands how I feel. I haven't been out with anyone since and can't ever see myself doing so. I know this sounds silly and unimportant but I'm so depressed.
Girl, age 17

D   I'm shy, she's shy

I'm a boy who fancies a girl, but I don't know how to go up to her and start a conversation. She's quite shy and doesn't really mix with people. I want to make friends, but I don't know how. I'm quite shy too so it makes it difficult for me. Every time I'm looking at her she always seems to be looking at me. Does this mean she fancies me too?
Boy, age 14

E   Suicidal feelings

I took an overdose last year—I didn't really want to kill myself, it was more a cry for attention. I was referred to a counsellor who told me I had coped with my problems very well. But recently, I find my suicidal feelings are emerging again. I was sexually abused by my brother and uncle when younger, but my family covered it up. I have confided my problems to my best friend, who has been brilliant. But she is moving and I don't know how I'll cope when she leaves.

Girl

F   Am I normal?

I need reassurance that I'm normal. I'm nearly 19, at college, and have never had a proper boyfriend. This doesn't bother me much, and in many ways I'm proud of myself, but when I hear of 15-year-olds (and younger) having sex and being capable of coping with the emotional problems, I feel so immature. Even though I'm attracted to certain boys and some of them appear to like me, I can never actually see myself having sex with them, although I do fantasize about it. I have never told anyone this before because most of my friends have been sexually active since before the age of consent (i.e. under 16). Popping into bed with boys meant nothing to them at all. I read in a problem page recently that people who are afraid of sex were either sexually abused as children or have suffered some other devastating trauma. Since neither of these apply to me, why do I always freeze up every time a boy I like makes an advance?

Girl, age 18

G   The condom split!

My girlfriend and I are both 15 and we recently had sex. The thing is, the condom split and we are both very worried about the consequences. We aren't quite sure what to do as, if she is pregnant, her mum and dad will both flip and probably stop us from seeing one another. I think my parents are more understanding and they'll probably listen but they certainly wouldn't let us go on seeing each other. We love one another and we don't want to be separated. Her period is due soon and we are going to wait and see, but if she does miss it and is pregnant, neither of us knows what to do.

Boy, age 15

H   I slept with my sister's boyfriend

I'm 16 and about four months ago I started seeing my sister's 26-year-old boyfriend. At the time I had sex with him I was only 15 which made matters worse. My sister caught us not long ago and in a way I'm glad she did. The fact that she's still with him hurts me a lot. Me and my sister still talk but it's not like it was before. I don't talk to him any more. He just called me a slag and told me never to go to his house again. It's not that I love him or anything, it's just that I feel used and dirty and slaggish. My sister didn't tell my parents because they would have gone berserk and it would have gone to court and everything. But I don't know what to do next. I hate myself for what I've done and I've thought about killing myself. It's only a matter of time so please help me before I do it.

Girl, age 16

I   I've got no freedom

My parents are messing up my life. I am 15 and I've started going out to night-clubs with friends. At first mum let me go on condition I was home by a certain time (far earlier than any of my friends, incidentally) but I didn't mind too much. Then mum found out that one of my friends hadn't told her mum where she was going. My mum then decided that I wasn't allowed out until this girl owned up! I've got no freedom at all and my parents just laugh when I tell them how unhappy I am.

Girl, age 15

J   My girlfriend pesters me about sex

I am afraid that I'm being pushed too far by my girlfriend. I am younger than her and she seems to expect a lot from me. She pesters me about sex, and every time I kiss her she pushes me further. I am afraid she might leave me because there is no sex in our relationship. Please help.

Boy

K   They won't leave me alone

My mum is on the verge of a nervous breakdown and my sister and stepdad say it's my fault. I know I'm moody and bad-tempered sometimes with my family and friends, but while my friends understand, my family doesn't. My sister and I argue and fight all the time, and I just wish my family would leave me alone. I've even thought about running away, but I can't bring myself to do it.

Girl

L   I want to have a baby

I had a abortion a year ago and although I thought it was the right decision to make at the time, now I feel so guilty and all I want is to have a child. My boyfriend says we're far too young (I'm 17 and he's 18) and, deep down, I know that he's right, but I can't help thinking that getting pregnant is the only way I'm ever going to be happy.

Girl, age 17

M   Bingeing is ruining my life

Every day I count calories and work out how much I've eaten, but sometimes I'm so weak-willed that I go mad and eat everything in sight, then I feel guilty and stick my fingers down my throat. I'm worried about going on holiday because of my eating habits.

Girl

N   My boyfriend's into porn

I recently discovered dirty videos hidden at my boyfriend's house. I confronted him and he said that they were only for a laugh and if he doesn't take them seriously, then why should I? But I'm so shocked that he could be like that. Should I forgive him?

Girl

You should have two 'problems' to work through the following questions with.

1   I want you to focus on the young person, rather than the problem. What do you imagine them to be like? Close your eyes and try to picture the young person who wrote this letter. Then jot down a few lines or draw a quick sketch to help you think of them as a real person, rather than an academic exercise.

2   Read the letter again. What problem or problems is this young person asking for help with?

For example:
M   Bingeing is ruining my life
This girl is asking for help to control her eating habits.

3   Behind the 'presenting problem' there lie a number of fears, hopes, anxieties, wishes and so on. Try to pin-point each of these underlying the problem in the letter, and write a sentence for each.

For example:
M   Bingeing is ruining my life
She is anxious about putting on weight.
She is afraid of the effect food might have on her.
She is worried about what other people might think if she goes on holiday—if they see her eating habits.
She wants to control what she eats and how she looks.
She fears that this bingeing is taking over her life, preventing her from doing things that she wants to like go on holiday.

4   Behind these fears, hopes, anxieties, wishes and so on, there often lie unmet needs. Try to pin-point these and write a sentence on each.

For example:
M   Bingeing is ruining my life
She needs to be in control of her life.
She needs to feel attractive and acceptable to others.

5   Now that you have explored the problem, see if you can make any links between the good news of Jesus Christ and this young person's situation. How can your response be good news to this young person?

Spend some time on this. Think back to the work you did looking at the impact of parental divorce in the lives of young people and how the gospel might start to interact with that.

It is important to realize that sometimes we are the good news to a young person. What I mean is that we are there, sent by God. We may be the active expression of his care for that young person, the answer to 'why doesn't God do anything then?'

Compared to a printed answer in an impersonal magazine, we should be good news in terms of offering on-going support to the young person. Rather than just suggesting they seek professional help, we can help them to find out what is available and, if necessary, go with them and be around as someone they can talk to about sorting the problem out as it goes along.

Jesus isn't a cure-all. We shouldn't just look for links in terms of needs God can meet, fears and anxieties he can dispel, hopes and wishes he can grant. Sometimes the good news is much more radical than that.

For example:

M   Bingeing is ruining my life

The good news is that she doesn't have to be in control of her life. For someone who is anorexic or bulimic, hearing about their guilt in regard to sin, and the Christian life of self-discipline with regard to temptation is not necessarily good news. These aspects, far from setting someone free from the self-destructive cycle of guilt and compulsive control, may just reinforce this, now with the added power of God in the role of condemner. This girl needs good news that will set her free from the prison of self-destruction as a way of coping with life.

Part of this good news is the acceptance that Christ offers (think of the woman caught in adultery and Christ's response), and that we offer as Christ's ambassadors. A root to her problem may be that she has only experienced love as conditional 'I am loveable if... I am slim.' If we are able to show her by our words and actions that we accept her unconditionally, she may come to believe that Christ accepts her too.

The good news is that this preoccupation with food which began as something that helped her to cope with her life, and has turned into something that rules her life, is not what life is all about. 'Man does not live by bread alone, but by every word that proceeds from the mouth of God.' The good news is that there is something much more important, something which doesn't take over your life but which fills your life with meaning and good things (love, joy, peace, patience, kindness, goodness, faithfulness, gentleness and self-control).

▧ TEENAGE PROBLEMS: A CASE-STUDY

INTRODUCTION

For this section you will need to have two sets of information:

◆ the views of the young people you work with about an issue

◆ some 'factual' information about that issue.

In order to get both of these you will need to do some homework:

◆ by compiling a questionnaire, asking the young people to complete it and looking at their answers

◆ by visiting your local library or Citizen's Advice Bureau and looking the subject up.

Both of these will take time, I realize, so this section will be much thinner than the others! I have my reasons for asking you to find this information yourself! And laziness on my part isn't the main one:

◆ By asking the young people you work with, you will be finding out more about them as a group, and what *they* think *now*—this will be much more interesting and useful to you in your youthwork than anything I could tell you about a group of teenagers in Oxford and what they thought at the time I was writing this!

◆ Similarly, information becomes out of date and irrelevant very quickly where teenagers are concerned, and you will be able to find out much more relevant stuff than I could supply. You should also discover a little about the resources that are available to you in your youthwork—vital local info!

I am telling you this at the start of the section, so you have a chance to plan in some time to do these bits of research—and so you're not under any illusions about being able to sit down and whiz through this section in an evening.

XERCISE

Below is lots of factual information about various 'teenage problems'. Read it all through, then use this information to choose a subject that interests you and which you think is relevant to the lives of the young people with whom you work.

Sex

Over the last forty years, the average age for someone's first sexual experience has dropped from twenty-one to seventeen.

Surveys suggest that between one in five and one in three young people under the age of sixteen have had sex.

One in ten people claim they were drunk when they lost their virginity.

By the age of eighteen a person will have watched on television 9,000 actual or suggested acts of sexual intercourse.

Crime

80 per cent of eleven to seventeen-year-olds are concerned by rising youth crime, and 60 per cent believe that the police and government are failing in their attempts to tackle the problem.

Almost two out of three young people claim to know someone in their age group who behaves badly or breaks the law.

93 per cent of young offenders caught by West Yorkshire Police are regular drug users. Only 6 per cenct of fifteen to twenty-four-year-olds had been charged with drugs-related offences, but many were spending between £150 and £600 a week on drugs with crime being their main source of income.

The number of juveniles aged under seventeen convicted of or cautioned for indictable offences fell by 37 per cent from 175,800 in 1980 to 109,000 in 1990.

Smoking

In 1993 just over one million eleven to fifteen-year-olds had at least tried a cigarette, 41 per cent of the age group. A quarter of a million, that is 8 per cent of the age group, considered themselves to be regular smokers.

According to statistics from 1994, 20 per cent of fifteen-year-old girls were regular smokers, a total of 56,000; 18 per cent of boys the same age were, a total of 53,000.

Solvent abuse

In 1990 there were 149 deaths from solvent sniffing. About one third died on what was probably their first attempt at sniffing.

One in ten secondary school age young people will try sniffing.

Anorexia and bulimia nervosa

Over 20,000 school age people suffer from these eating disorders (one in three of all sufferers fall in this age group).

10 per cent of sufferers will die from either the results of starvation or suicide.

Between 5 and 10 per cent of sufferers are male.

Alcohol

1,000 under-fifteen-year-olds are admitted to hospital each year with acute alcohol poisoning.

35,000 under-sixteen-year-olds drink more alcohol than the safe limits recommended for adults.

The most common cause of death for sixteen to twenty-year-olds is from car accidents where drink was involved.

Suicide

Every two hours someone in Britain kills themselves, and somebody tries to take their own life every two and a half minutes. Among teenagers, suicide is the second highest cause of death.

The earliest age for suicide is twelve; suicide rates increase sharply at age fifteen.

Actual suicides are more common among boys; while attempted suicides are more common among girls (by as much as four times).

The Samaritans report an 83 per cent rise in suicides by young men aged

between sixteen and twenty-four in 1992 (412 suicides) as compared with 1982 (262 suicides). Over the same period the suicide rate for young women has dropped by 43 per cent, although they do make more attempted suicides.

Teenage pregnancies

Women under twenty from the most deprived areas are six times more likely to have an unwanted pregnancy than those from affluent suburbs.

One in four teenage pregnancies from deprived areas are likely to be terminated by an abortion; whilst two-thirds of those from affluent areas are likely to abort (these figure are based on NHS hospital abortions only).

In England and Wales more than 4,500 girls under the age of fifteen become pregnant each year.

Drugs

A survey by the Institute for the Study of Drug Dependence in 1992 showed that up to a third of young people have tried illegal drugs or solvents by the age of twenty.

One in four young adults (around 2 million people) are likely to have tried cannabis.

One in ten are likely to have tried amphetamines.

One in ten are likely to have tried magic mushrooms.

One in ten are likely to have tried ecstasy.

One in ten are likely to have tried LSD.

One in ten are likely to have tried amyl nitrate (poppers).

One in one hundred are likely to have tried heroin or cocaine.

Aids

One in three twelve to fifteen-year-olds agree with the statement 'Aids is only a problem if I get it.'

Now focus on your chosen subject. Spend a few minutes reflecting on why you have chosen this particular issue. How do you react to the 'facts'? Do they surprise, worry or reassure you?

Is there a subject you would rather work on that is not covered above? If so, then use that instead. The aim is for you to investigate something of interest and relevance to your work.

This section is really just one long exercise. The 'facts' were just to get you started. There is no feedback for this exercise, because it would be impossible for me to write something that covered anything you might do. My advice to you is *just do it!*

Here goes:

A Write a questionnaire to use with the young people that you work with on your chosen subject.

Think carefully about what your aim is—what is it that you want to find out?

◆ How much information do they know about the subject?

◆ How much experience do they have of the subject?

◆ What do they think about the subject—their views and so on?

◆ Where would they go for help on the subject?

Phrase your questions carefully—think about how you want people to answer:

◆ yes or no

◆ multiple choice

◆ space for one word/one sentence/a paragraph

It is important to have a logical sequence to the questions, starting with more straightforward ones and perhaps finishing with more personal or complex ones.

Think about how you introduce the questionnaire to the young people—particularly the issue of confidentiality. Tell them who will see their answers, whether they need to put their names on and so on.

Think about how many people you are going to ask to fill it in—will you be able to use the volume of information you might get?

Think about who will be answering the questions and use language appropriate for their age and ability.

Will you be there to help them answer the questions, or do all the instructions need to be on the sheet?

Once you are happy with your questionnaire, photocopy it and give it to the young people whose answers you want. I have found that they are usually quite happy to help in this way, and even enjoy filling them in!

B Do some background research on this issue yourself.

The local phone book may be a good place to start—lists of specialist organizations can usually be found near the front—why not ring one up and see if they can send you some information?

The local library is a good resource— you'll be surprised to find books in the reference section with useful information. Again, they can often put you in touch with local support groups.

Ask other youthworkers, social workers or police for information.

Start to build up a better overview of the subject. You might want to look out for newspaper and magazine articles that deal with the issue as well.

C   You now have two sets of information:

◆ from local young people

◆ from research.

Read through all you have collected so far, and start to put it together. Ask yourself the following questions:

◆ Is this subject a real issue in the lives of the young people?

◆ How does this issue interact with the process of growing up?

◆ Do these young people have enough information to make informed choices in their lives on this subject?

◆ Do these young people know where to go for help on this subject?

◆ Do these young people know what they think or believe about this subject?

◆ As a Christian youthworker, do you want to respond to any of their expressed or unexpressed needs on this subject?

◆ What light does the gospel bring to bear on this subject?

D   Given your answers to the questions above, what will you do in your role as a Christian youthworker?

Do you want to plan a piece of 'issue-based' work with this group of young people? If so, what are your aims, and how will you go about doing this?

Do you want to change any working practices where you do your youthwork? If so, what are your aims and how will you go about doing this?

Do you want to see a change in provision for these young people? If so, what are your aims and how will you go about doing this?

Do you want to raise awareness in other sections of the community about this issue? If so, what are your aims and how will you go about doing this?

Make use of all the hard work you have done—remember you are not on your own out there. There are plenty of resources you can tap into for anything from organizing a discussion to campaigning for a change in the law!

That's it for 'the outside world'— well done for making it this far. Only one more chapter to go!

WORSHIP AND YOUNG PEOPLE

8

Pete Ward

WHAT IS WORSHIP?

INTRODUCTION

I don't think that we can help young people to worship if we haven't explored worship for ourselves. There was one occasion when I was talking with a group of youth leaders about the amazing experiences young people often report when they start to worship God for the first time. I mentioned how young people I have known have been dramatically touched by the Spirit of God so that they really feel God's presence as a warm glow or as a joyful feeling which wells up inside them. One of the youth leaders immediately responded, 'How can I introduce young people to such an experience if I haven't myself met God in that way?'

This is a crucial question and it goes right to the heart of leading worship for young people. I want to reply by saying two things.

First, worship is very personal and individual. Everybody

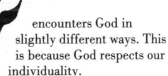

encounters God in slightly different ways. This is because God respects our individuality.

Secondly, we can all learn more about worship but there's no point getting up-tight about not experiencing this, that or the other when we worship. We need to start where we are at by exploring our own experience of God in worship.

If we want to help young people to worship God then we need to be prepared to do some work on worship ourselves. This section concentrates on your own experience of worship. The following exercise is designed to help you to do this.

145

EXERCISE

This exercise is based on remembering an experience of worship which you have had in the past. Take a little time to think about one particular occasion when you were involved in worshipping God. A good way to get into this kind of exercise is to start with some of the details. These could include:

◆ First think about one particular time when you felt that you were genuinely worshipping God.

◆ Where you were when this worship happened? Spend a few minutes thinking about this place. Try to recall what this place was like. If you can concentrate on senses like smell and touch as well as sight you will get a more realistic memory.

◆ Go through in your mind the way things happened during this time of worship so that you have a good idea what went on.

◆ Try to concentrate on what you felt as you were worshipping.

Take as long as you think is necessary to remember this experience of worship. When you feel that you have recalled this event to its fullest, answer the following questions by writing a short note in your folders. These questions are meant to help with your own reflection on the experience of worship.

1   What role did your feelings play in this time of worship?

2   Was there something or someone that helped you to start to worship? Was your worship sparked off by anything in particular?

3   Were you with other people or on your own when you worshipped God? How important to the experience was it that you were on your own or with other people?

FEEDBACK

1   For most of us, the 'feel' of worship is tremendously important. Some young people I know will come out of a church service and say something like, 'It was great! God was there.' I think they realize that God is in fact always with us, but something has happened during this worship time which has meant that they have encountered God in a fresh and exciting way. In general what they mean by this is that they have experienced the presence of God during the service. The worship time was genuine and real because it felt right.

I know myself that I want to come out of a church service with a sense that I have been touched by God in some way. The best worship times are those that leave me feeling that I have been changed in some way. Somehow the worship has made the coming week look better and more exciting. Before the worship time I was going in one direction and after it I was heading in another. Meeting God in worship turns me around. It's probably for this reason that I find it hard to imagine a worship time which does not involve my feelings. I sense that I have been changed by meeting God.

2   But worship is a great deal more than what we feel. When I think back to worship which has meant something to me I have usually found that a key factor has been that something has sparked me to worship. Sometimes this is a passage from the Bible, at other times it is the communion service itself, sometimes it is the memory of something that has happened or the anticipation of something that is to come. The point about these situations and what prompts me to worship is that they all point to God. The letter of John makes this very clear.

This is what love is: it is not that we loved God, but that he loved us and sent his Son to be the means by which our sins are forgiven.

1 John 4:10 (GNB)

Worship is a reaction to the original action of God in loving us. We worship God because this is the right human response to the one who has created and redeemed the world. We have not initiated the encounter in any way—it is God who has made the first move. It is always God's word to us that sparks us to worship.

3   Getting together with people seems to be a crucial factor in worship. It is perfectly possible to worship God on your own but in my experience it is when I am with a group that I seem to meet God in the most significant ways. Other people inspire me by their willingness to be open to God in worship. On many occasions I get to a worship time feeling very cold and quite distant from God. Other people somehow help me to defrost slowly and open up to God. Sometimes they do this by the things they say as they lead us in worship, other times it's just the mere fact of being with other people who I care for and respect that makes the difference.

INSTRUCTIONS

Before reading the next section you need to read Psalm 40.

 NPUT

In my Good News Bible, Psalm 40 is called 'A Song of Praise'. The Psalm divides neatly into five sections, each one dealing with a different aspect of worship. The first part of this section has concentrated on the experience of worship. Psalm 40 is also filled with the experience of worship but a close study of this passage reveals that the person writing the Psalm has a broad view of how worship works out in practice.

Worship is about the way that God has rescued us in the past (vv. 1–3), but it is also about a willingness to place our future in God's hands (v. 5). Worship is about telling of what God has done when the congregation meets together (vv. 9–10), but it is also about hearing God's word and doing it (vv. 6–8). Above all though, worship is the act of putting our trust in God who loves us and keeps us safe (v. 11). Here are my reflections on each of these sections. Use them as an aid to your own thinking about worship.

TELLING THE STORY (vv. 1–3)

The person who wrote this song had been through a tough ordeal. He (I assume a man wrote this Psalm) certainly had a story to tell. Young people at one time used to talk about life as being 'the pits'. To be trapped in a hole with no real prospect of getting out is common to many people's experience.

But this person was able to wait patiently for God who set him 'safely on a rock'. This is a story about being rescued. Christian worship will nearly always need to centre around the way that Jesus rescued us by his death on the cross. This is one reason why I find the communion service to be so helpful because it focuses on the death of Christ.

A SENSE OF PURPOSE (vv. 4–5)

We can get excited about being Christians because God has done so many good things for us. We have not only been rescued, we have also been included in the amazing plans which God has for the world. Rejoicing in a sense of purpose is an essential part of Christian worship. Young people are also greatly in need of a sense of purpose in life. It is primarily in worshipping God that they find a sense of direction and hope. This hope is in direct contrast to what is offered to young people by a materialist society. Idolatry is real and it leads young people to an empty life which lacks direction and dignity. Others may worship idols but we resolve to worship God.

HEARING AND DOING (vv. 6–8)

God is not really interested in religious rituals. The trappings of religion, even the Christian religion, are in danger of being meaningless. Instead God has given us ears to hear him and he wants us to obey what he tells us to do. The heart of our worship must be a willingness to do the will of God. The true focus of worship is not in church, it is in daily life. Young people need to get hold of this idea that worship is doing. We need to realize that what happens in church is not the be-all and end-all of worship. We can only do this when we find ways to value and support young people in their day-to-day lives.

TELLING THE STORY (vv. 9–10)

The person writing this Psalm is concerned to point out what God has been doing in his life and in the lives of those around him. Witness and testimony are an important part of a gathering for worship. Like the Psalmist we must say that we 'will never stop telling'. When young people get together to worship they will need to have space to tell their stories so that they too can feel that they can tell of what God has done for them.

TRUST IN GOD (v. 11)

In the end, our worship involves a reliance on God for our safety. There is something child-like about this willingness to trust God. Young people will find it hard to put their lives into God's hands. Everything about their upbringing and the culture around them says that self-reliance is the only way forward. Trust in God is tough if everyone you have trusted in the past has let you down. Nevertheless, real worship starts with trust in a God who is uniquely worthy of that trust.

LEARNING TO WORSHIP

INPUT

Everybody needs to learn to worship. Most of us learn the skills of worshipping by being around Christian people when they are praying or singing and somehow we pick it up. For many young people who are outside the church this is impossible. Most young people feel very uncomfortable in church and do not mix easily with people who go to church. Passing on the skills of worship becomes a real problem when you are working with those who do not fit socially into a church or even a church youth group.

If you are a youthworker contacting young people who do not fit very easily into church there is a real need to create a place where they can start to learn to worship slowly. A full-blown alternative worship service in a church may not be the best place for this to happen. At Oxford Youth Works we have discovered that young people who have had no church background find even an alternative worship service, like JOY, to be a little overpowering. We have therefore developed a two-stage approach to worship in our work. The first stage we call Worship and the second is JOY which happens once a month in a local church and is led by young people themselves.

The two stages, Worship and JOY, have similar styles but they differ greatly in their emphasis. Worship recognizes the fact that most people who come are learning how to worship. The leaders involved in running Worship play a fairly active role in each of the weekly sessions, creating a series of easy-to-join-in-with worship sessions which lead people from relatively little experience of meeting God in worship through to a more regular prayer and spritual life. JOY on the

other hand is a committed group of people who meet weekly on a Sunday evening to worship God and plan the monthly service. Worship is designed for people from fourteen to about eighteen whilst JOY is for those from around seventeen to about twenty-five.

This section is focused on the first stage of this process. If you want to know more about JOY then I refer you to my book *Worship and Youth Culture* where the first year of JOY is described along with some of the things we did in services.

 EXERCISE

Take fifteen minutes to write an answer to the following question in your folder:

In your situation would a halfway-house worship session such as 'Worship' help you in your work? Give reasons for your answer.

INPUT

PLANNING WORSHIP

Last week my turn came round to take Worship. In planning the time I had two aims in mind. The first was that I wanted to talk about sin. The second was that I wanted to run a worship session which did not involve using a guitar or any corporate singing. I will call the session 'Is it a sin?' Here is my plan for this session.

'IS IT A SIN?'

A plan for one Worship session to last one hour

The setting. This week at Worship there was a mixed group of about twenty-five adults and young people. We were all sitting on the floor in a basement room which is three times as long as it is wide. The group fits well into this space and it felt cosy without being too cramped.

Introduction. I was aware that 'sin' could be a tricky subject for the group to deal with. So I started with a short incident I had observed that week in school. I explained that each week I go to Oxford School to help a group of young people learn to play rock music. This particular lunchtime I was helping with a drum lesson. On the drums was a rather overweight young boy and he was struggling because it was his very first time on a full drum kit. Just as my friend started to drum an older lad put his head through an open window and yelled across the classroom, 'Fatso, Oi Fatso. I'm gonna smash your face in when you get out. Fatso.' I don't think this guy knew my friend on the drums. So this verbal assault came from out of the blue.

Having told this brief story I explained to the group at Worship that I had puzzled over what I should think of this guy's actions towards my friend. I was interested to know if God had a view about this insulting and threatening kind of behaviour. 'What should we make of this?' I said, 'Is this behaviour a *mistake*? Is it just an *accident*? Is it perhaps a *stupid action*? Or should we say that it was a *sin*?' I made it clear that I wanted the group at Worship to make their mind up about this incident and also about a number of other situations which I would pass on to them as the Worship time went on. They were to

divide up into groups of around seven or eight people and prepare for a moral debate.

Each group was given four sheets of paper. On these sheets I had written in large bold letters:

- ◆ MISTAKE
- ◆ ACCIDENT
- ◆ STUPID ACTION
- ◆ SIN

Each group was given three or four minutes to discuss a situation and then they were asked to hold up one of these sheets to show what they had decided in their group. The situations that I asked them to consider were:

- ◆ The attempt by a character in an Australian soap to get off with her sister's long-standing boyfriend.
- ◆ The James Bulger murder trial.
- ◆ A person who had collected sponsor money and then used the money for themselves.
- ◆ The Duchess of York's toe-sucking incident.
- ◆ A person at a party offering a tablet to someone who subsequently goes into a coma.

I introduced each of these topics one at a time and then ensued a time of heated argument. The young people launched into the discussions with a great deal of enthusiasm. After each short period of discussion I gave them thirty seconds to make a decision and then I called for a vote, at which point they held up their sheets depending on what they had decided. After each vote I introduced the next situation and the process continued.

When we had discussed each of the situations I gave a short message: I was surprised at how frequently the sin sheet was chosen by each of the groups. I remarked on this and then said that 'sin' was something which Jesus talked about a great deal. I then said that on one occasion Jesus was eating with some religious leaders when these religious people asked his disciples why they hung out with sinners. Jesus replied, 'People who are well do not need a doctor, but only those who are sick.' This incident is found in Luke 5:29–32 but I retold the story in my own words. I then went on to point out that it is easy to point the finger at other people and say they are sinners but each one of us does things that are wrong. We are all sinners. I was anxious to make it plain that I was not excluding myself from this fact and so I confessed to the group that when I was a teenager I had taken some sponsorship money that I had collected.

Prayer. I then told the group that I wanted them to spend a short while meditating. I was going to play some music and read a short passage from the Bible over the top of it. I told the group that they did not have to try to follow the whole passage if they didn't want to. It was OK to take a phrase or a line and think about that if they wanted to. In the event I read the passage twice. I played a track from an 'Enigma' tape which had some Gregorian chant on it and I read over the top of this Psalm 36 which contrasts the person who plots wickedness with the love and protection of the Lord.

When the tape had finished I wanted the group to continue to pray. I was concerned that this worship time should leave a good deal of space for the group to reach out to God in their own way. Talk of sin is heavy and the best way to process this is to reach out to Jesus who promises to be a doctor to

the sick. So I explained that I was going to play another tape and those who wanted to pray could stick around and those who wanted to leave I asked to go quietly. This tape was relatively short but it was again ambient atmospheric music. Slowly the room emptied and when everyone had gone the worship time was over.

EXERCISE

Imagine that you are in the situation where there are fifteen young people who are asking you to help them to worship. They know nothing about the Christian faith, but they want to learn. Your task is to plan a worship time for this group.

Planning this session and writing it up in your notebook should take about forty minutes.

The worship time should be based on a real-life situation that you think the group will readily identify with. If you regularly plan worship sessions for young people then decide from the start to do something new or different. In my case I left out singing songs which usually form a large part of Worship. The worship should not last more than an hour and it should include:

◆ **a simple retelling of a Bible story**

◆ **some ideas for prayer**

◆ **a time for the young people themselves to get involved in discussion**

◆ **space either using silence or music or some other method where the young people can be encouraged to open up to God.**

EEDBACK

Having planned your worship time, it would be good to actually see if it works. If you can think of a group that might want you to do something different for them, why don't you try it out? It doesn't have to be a group of young people. You could try your plan out on a fellowship group or invite a few friends round to experience your work first hand.

It's a good idea to leave some time to talk about the session with the group so that you can learn what you did well and what you can improve.

You may have found this exercise to be quite challenging. I shouldn't worry about this. Planning worship is very difficult, especially when you do not know the group you are going to be working with. As a rule of thumb however I would say that the simplest plans are nearly always the best. Creativity in planning worship is a skill which takes time to develop.

▌ WORSHIP AND YOUTH CULTURE

NPUT

The following 'Input' is an article I wrote which was published in the *Church of England Newspaper* in reply to a review of my book *Worship and Youth Culture*. The reviewer pointed out that in many churches the evening service is starting to lose its popularity. Taking this as my starting point I argue for alternative worship which arises from the culture of young people to be taken seriously as the end point for outreach to those young people who are currently not reached by the church.

O ur Sunday evening service may well be empty or redundant, but this is in no way a reason for setting up an alternative worship service. We must start with young people themselves rather than a gap in the church's programme. Mission amongst young people is not about keeping the church going, it is about the extension of the Kingdom of God.

In considering the value of alternative worship it is this gospel or 'mission' perspective which must predominate, because alternative worship finds its origins in those who are currently outside the church. In other words it is the result of long-term Christian mission. The JOY service in Oxford has come from years of friendship-based outreach to young people in the local community. The majority of the young people who worship at JOY have come to faith through the caring relationships developed with them by Oxford Youth Works staff and volunteers. Adults have spent time befriending young people and learning about their lives and culture. The worship which has evolved is 'alternative' precisely because it takes the question of culture seriously.

We must recognize that we live in a pluralistic society which is becoming increasingly divided. The middle-class culture of the church is just one sub-culture amongst many others. The problem is that the Anglican tradition, and those of other churches, of common prayer, rests on an assumption about a shared English culture which no longer holds water. This is as much true of evangelical charismatic worship as it is of *The Book of Common Prayer* or other church liturgies. All assume that people who do not share the cultural frameworks which operate in the church will somehow fit in. In fact some would say that this is 'good' for them. Young people we are told must be 'churched'. By this we mean, whether we realize it or not, that they should be socialized into the middle-class attitudes, values and behaviour that predominate in the church.

Ironically in the wider society there is an incredible growth in spirituality. Most young people believe in God, a good many pray. My own experience is that Jesus is very attractive to young people, but what they can't cope with is the cultural assumptions of the church. Alternative worship is an attempt to address this very

problem and the way we do this is by taking youth culture seriously. To do this we need to make visits to youth events which happen outside the life of the church such as 'raves' and 'concerts' and sporting events.

Christian youthwork beyond the fringes of the church must be inspired by a theology of mission which is willing to wrestle with context. Part of the reason why the church is so out of touch with young people is because we have consistently failed to take this message on board. We expect young people to come to us rather than being willing to meet them on their own home territory. Thus mission has been replaced by missions, i.e. events to which people are invited. How can we ever expect to understand young people, let alone identify with them, if we are not willing to spend time with them in places where they feel at home and comfortable? It is only when we are with people in these kinds of places that we can begin to discover how Jesus makes sense in their cultural world, we cannot do this from a distance. Being with young people is the starting point for a contextualized sharing of the gospel, i.e. one which attempts to make concrete the message of Jesus within the cultural world of the young people with whom you are in contact. Alternative worship happens when these young people respond to Jesus who is real and makes sense within their cultural world.

Alternative Worship, however, is not just about raves. Youth culture itself is extremely diverse and always changing. If we latch on to 'rave' as the answer we again miss the point. Alternative worship comes about when particular groups of young people start to express their love for Christ in ways that make sense to them. True alternative worship services will be as varied as the youth cultures from which they arise. Young people are the generative force behind this new wave of creativity in the church. It is not the case that a few trendy church leaders can lay on a service for young people based on what is happening elsewhere in the country, even if we are inspired by the lofty realms of Sheffield.

There is no short cut to getting to know Jimmy and John and Sandra who hang out in the shopping centre and spending enough time with them so that you can share Jesus with them in a real and moving way. As Jimmy and John and Sandra read the Bible and express their faith in Christ in their own terms alternative worship begins to grow. Such worship is 'alternative' precisely because it is based on cultural expressions which are different from those at present predominating within the church.

EXERCISE

You have heard what I think. Now what do you make of alternative worship for young people? Here are a few questions which should get you thinking about this issue. Take about thirty minutes to make notes on these questions in your notebook.

1 **Bearing in mind what I have said in the article, are there reasons you can think of why young people in your local area should have a service which is specially designed for them?**

2 **If you were setting up a service, how would you help the young people to take part in the planning of the service?**

3 **What kind of service would be best for young people in your local area who do not at present go to church?**

FEEDBACK

1 Alternative worship based on youth culture is currently a very controversial area. Many people feel that a separate service for young people is against the 'family feel' of the local church. Some would say that young people should be part of a wider body which can offer maturity and a diversity of backgrounds. I would say that in the long run this should be the case. A divided church is ultimately an offence to the gospel.

However the key thing is that we recognize that young people live 'culturally' in a very different world to that of the church. The first priority needs to be a willingness to let young people express their faith in their own cultural terms. The unity of the church and the fact that Christ is Lord of all needs to be a long-term aim of our work. When a service is up and running the older generation can begin to appreciate and learn from the young people. When the young people are valued in this way they may in turn begin to respond to the positive messages being put over by the adults. In this way alternative worship is a step along the way to a more diverse and yet a culturally richer church.

2   Working with young people to create an act of worship is very important. In fact, I would say that this is at the heart of alternative worship. One way to do this is to get groups of young people working on music, words, the sermon and so on. These small working groups might take a month or two to come up with something. After a period working together, the service can be put together. When you first get things going you should expect that the young people will need a good deal of help and support. Adult leaders who can be around and help with the planning and then the practical problems of setting up a service are very important. The crucial thing is to allow young people enough freedom and space to make the service their own.

3   If you start with the interests and concerns of the young people that you are working with then the service will be relevant and meaningful to them. It is wrong to try and guess what they would like and then lay it on for them. This is especially true when it comes to the music used in the service. I have found that the best way to get good music going is to encourage the young people to write it themselves. If however you have a group that are not musical then get them to choose music that they like. One idea I have found to be very helpful is to use recorded music from well-known bands. Once again the young people should choose the music where possible.

SACRAMENTS AND SYMBOLS

NPUT

Many churches are starting to experiment with new kinds of worship for young people. At the root of this new movement in the church is the creative use of symbols in worship. Some of these symbols come from Christian tradition—for example the use of a church building or the bread and wine of the communion service—whilst some of the symbols are drawn from youth culture itself, for example, rock music, dancing and so on.

As youthworkers we need to realize that symbols are a rich source of inspiration and blessing for young people when they are used right. This section looks at the way that symbols work in worship. The following extract looks at the importance of symbols—in particular, the regular symbols of communion and baptism which I refer to as sacraments.

The following is an extract from *Worship and Youth Culture* published by HarperCollins.

Symbols are a part of our everyday lives. We all know that a red triangle on a road sign means that we have to beware of something, or that when red is showing on the traffic light we must stop. Young people also regularly use symbols in the way that they create their sense of group identity. Wearing a particular pair of Nike baseball boots for instance immediately places you in a different group to the person who wears a pair of Dr Martens. Christian worship is also highly symbolic. The most common symbol is the bread and wine used in the Communion; water is also used in Baptism. But symbolic actions, gestures, and words are so central to whatever we do when we worship that we sometimes fail to realise that they are in fact symbols. We will ordinarily kneel or bow our heads to pray, or sing songs about Jesus the Lamb, stand up when the minister walks into Church or simply shake hands with people during the service without thinking too much about the symbolic meaning behind these things.

The use of symbols in our worship has become a natural part of our behaviour.

They are a part of our shared Church culture. When young people start to experiment with new forms of worship they will also need to use symbols. Some they will bring from their own culture e.g. the sight of a DJ standing behind a pair of record decks in Church is symbolic of a Rave. Other symbols will be ones already used by the Church which have been adapted to suit the culture of the young people, e.g. receiving the bread and the wine in a communion service whilst listening to a rock band playing.

A CHRISTIAN APPROACH TO SYMBOLS

Symbols used in worship may come from youth culture or from the culture of the church but the crucial factor is that the symbols that we use speak of Christ. In fact a Christian approach to symbols will always start with the idea of Jesus himself being the true sign or symbol of God's activity in the world.

The good news of the New Testament is about God becoming a human being. God became flesh and blood; a man called Jesus. As John says, 'The Word became a human being and, full of grace and truth, lived among us. We saw his glory, the glory which he received as the Father's only Son' (John 1:14, GNB). In John's Gospel, Jesus and the things that he did are talked about as signs of God's presence amongst us. This fact is crucially important when we are talking about the way that we use symbols in our worship. Jesus is the most important sign or symbol of God's presence and activity in the world. The fact that God used the everyday life of a human being to speak to us is very important because it shows how seriously he takes our humanity and our need to experience his 'spiritual' presence through physical 'symbols'. St Athanasius writing in the third century AD puts it like this:

Men had turned from the contemplation of God above, and were looking for Him in the opposite direction, down among created things and things of sense. The Saviour of us all, the Word of God in His great love took to Himself a body and moved as Man among men, meeting their senses, so to speak, half way. He became Himself an object for the senses, so that those who were seeking the Father through sensible things might apprehend the Father through the works which He, the Word of God, did in the body.

St Athanasius puts his finger on it here, God meets us in ways that we can understand and this means the world of physical signs and symbols. But Jesus when he left his disciples realized that they would need a continuing sign of his presence with them and so at the Last Supper he showed them how he wanted to be remembered in the breaking of bread and in the cup of wine.

SACRAMENTS

The Christian church recognizes that some symbols used in worship are special. Jesus gave us the Lord's Supper and invited us to continue to remember his death by repeating the actions of eating bread and drinking wine. Baptism and marriage are similarly endorsed in the Gospels when Jesus takes part in them. To call these symbols sacraments is one way continually to remind ourselves that they are special. But there is also the fact that these sacraments are a place where God promises to meet us. Other symbols may be used by the Spirit to inspire us, but the sacraments are unique because God promises to be with us when we take part in them.

Christians we know are divided over the meaning of the sacraments. We disagree about baptism and we are disunited in the interpretation of the communion. It's not my intention to presume to try and sort these difficulties out here. Even if I could get my mind round all of the issues and arguments I think it's best that people solve this one within their own church setting and tradition. However I do want to make a strong plea for alternative worship to take seriously the use of the sacraments. It's been our experience that regular communion with a group of young people has been a constant source of strength and encouragement. There is a strange sense in which these kinds of actions take you to another dimension of Christian experience. It is not just the fact that the communion service connects us to every other Christian community, it also unites us together in a 'symbolic' way with each other. We seem to get close to each other when we take communion. But communion is also, at the same time, a way to meet God in a very personal and deep way. Why this is so I think we can to some extent leave to a more theological discussion. I simply want to say that Christian worship for young people which neglects this area will inevitably be turning its back on one of the most precious and spiritually enriching resources which are open to it. Indeed communion and baptism were gifts given us by Christ to help us grow in the faith. So we should not be surprised when young people find them to be helpful in their lives, because that is what they were meant to be.

 **EXERCISE**

 **FEEDBACK**

Symbols are very important to young people. This exercise is designed to help you to think creatively about the way that symbols can be used in worship.

Your task is to lead a prayer time in a local service. Ideally you should do this exercise with a group of young people. I realize not everyone will be able to get together with a group to do this sort of thing very easily. If you decide you should work on your own, all is not lost—this exercise can still help you to learn about worship.

The prayer time must be based around visual images which you have to set to music.

The prayer time should last no more than ten minutes.

For the purposes of this exercise all copyright on photos in magazines or in newspapers have been miraculously waved. So you can use any image you can find. (*NOTE:* This is not the case in real life. Photos are subject to copyright and you must pay to use them even in a church service.)

You have one slide projector and a tape recorder.

In your notebook, script out the prayer time, giving directions for the music, the pictures and the words. You should spend about one hour on this exercise.

If you get the chance, try out the prayer time on a group of people and get their reactions to it. Include some of their comments in your folder.

I hope you found this kind of prayer time exciting to plan and if you got as far as actually presenting the material I have to say well done. I hope that this has given you some encouragement to carry on experimenting with worship.

FOR A BETTER WORLD

Richard Adams and Phil Wells

A discussion-leading-to-action guide for those who want to take informed social action

£8.00
ISBN 0 7459 2682 7

AN INTRODUCTION TO CHURCH COMMUNICATION

Richard Thomas

Just the training book ministers and publicity officers need to do the vital task of church communication

£10.00
ISBN 0 7459 2886 2

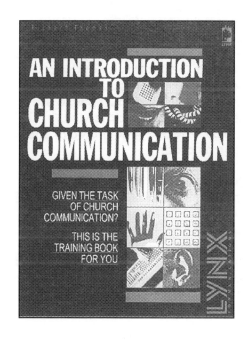

11